THE
plume
ANTHOLOGY OF
poetry
4

edited by Daniel Lawless

MADHAT PRESS
ASHEVILLE, NORTH CAROLINA

MadHat Press
MadHat Incorporated
PO Box 8364, Asheville, NC 28814

The material in this anthology is selected from
PlumePoetry.com
by Editor Daniel Lawless
with the editorial assistance of
Marc Vincenz & F. J. Bergmann

The Library of Congress has assigned
this edition a Control Number of
2015936763

ISBN 978-1-941196-28-1 (paperback)

Book layout and design by F. J. Bergmann
Cover design by Marc Vincenz

PlumePoetry.com
MadHat-Press.com

Tout ce qui arrive est à la fois naturel et inconcevable.
—Cioran, *Ecartèlement*

"*Plume*'s apparent lack of a narrow editorial policy (except a fondness for interesting poems) makes for lots of strange bedfellows, but what was the last time that was a bad idea?"
~ *Billy Collins*

"Of all the things that might claim one's attention, and they are in the multitudes! *Plume* is well worth making time for since it isn't just another magazine. Its difference? Wonderful work, on the edge, room for play and dash, new forms, a great discerning editor in Danny Lawless!"
~ *Tess Gallagher*

"*Plume* is one of the most exciting, eclectic gatherings of writers on the web. Editor Daniel Lawless has a knack for putting together voices that create surprising neighborhoods of words, related in complex ways that only gradually reveal themselves. It's one of very few webzines that I always read."
~ *Chase Twichell*

"*Plume* is rapidly becoming one of the best places in America to read poetry, online and in print, thanks to the untiring efforts of Danny Lawless. It's where to find dazzling work by new and established writers, and, thanks to the new technology, it is available instantly to readers by the millions. *Plume* proves once more that poetry is essential to our lives, and that 'Men die every day for want of what is found in it.'"
~ *Grace Schulman*

"*Plume* continues to publish amazing poets in beautiful formats—both online and in-print. The magazine has an exciting vision, embracing a broad gamut of poetries, including collaborations. The work has a consistently intriguing quality about the joys and unsettling aspects of being alive."
~ *Denise Duhamel*

"*Plume* is a new force in the poetry world, bringing together, in its online zine and in this anthology, a unique, eclectic and impressive group of poets."
~ *Rae Armantrout*

"I've never seen a literary magazine become so important so quickly. I have no idea how Daniel Lawless does it, but I dare anyone to find another journal that contains 1) the high quality of the individual poems, 2) the wide range of voices and styles, and 3) the large number of leading voices in contemporary American poetry. I would love to see all these poets in the same room, but I'll take them here, all in the same book."
~ *Jim Daniels*

"I usually hate to read poems on the computer but *Plume* has changed my mind. It is attractive, well-edited, and possesses the compelling virtue of being concise—not too many poems, not too few. Since I always end up wanting to print out one or two, I'm grateful for Danny Lawless's equally exciting, good-looking, and well-chosen, *Plume* anthologies."
~ *Lawrence Raab*

"*Plume* is a gathering place where strangers become old friends. Each issue is a celebration of images and words that touch the heart and bind us together as community."
~ *Lawrence Matsuda*

"The first word I remember using to describe Danny Lawless's online *Plume* was the word elegant. And now I discover that the word derives from a Latin verb for *to select*. *Plume* endeavors to select and showcase— yes, elegantly—the best poems of the twenty-first century. *Plume* not only encourages, it honors poetry."
~ *Ron Smith*

"*Plume* is a gem—in the rare-and-wondrous-find sense. Each issue is a hand-plucked, precisely curated composition, tended with great care, full of mystery, and delivering batches of the freshest, most provocative, and necessary writing around. Danny Lawless's vision is exquisite."
~ *Lia Purpura*

"Though I've been known to shy away from online publications, I'm an avid reader of *Plume*, a beautifully designed monthly periodical featuring an international selection of works by some of today's best poets. Hard to beat that."
~ *William Trowbridge*

"Plume (Noun): An anthology or journal of fine writing edited with passion and immaculate attention to detail.
"Plume (Verb): To erupt with energy, enthusiasm and poetic spirit. To dazzle.
"Derivative of Plume: Plumelike (Adjective): As fine as down and as lively as peacock feathers.
"Origins of *Plume*: American, but with an internationalist bent, some time during the 2000s."
~ *John Kinsella*

Daniel Lawless has a gift for publishing poets who not only represent the breadth and depth at which the art is practiced today, but who together make—how to say it?—a feisty crowd, their proximity in the pages of *Plume* creating all sorts of surprising angles of vision. There's nothing rote in Daniel's editorial choices, nothing of what Emerson called "a foolish consistency." His assemblages of poems, images, and editorial musings have a hand-crafted, one-of-a-kind feel. That's why there's ever cause for celebration when another *Plume*, whether online or in print, makes its way into the world.
~ *Clare Rossini*

"*Plume* magazine is an anomaly of taste: any literary dwelling that can shelter under one roof a family of poets as distantly related as Rae Armantrout, James Richardson, Kim Addonizio, Jorie Graham, Linda Pastan, G.C. Waldrep, Grace Schulman, Carl Phillips, Sharon Olds, Billy Collins, and more, must be both capacious and *odd*. What in the world unites these writers, one thinks? And then one reads an issue of *Plume* with the dawning recognition what they have in common is Danny Lawless, the founder and editor of this superb new journal. Lawless has the audacity to choose the poets he loves, and believes are writing *good* poetry, no matter on what wildly disparate branch of the family tree he finds them. And then he gets these poets to send him poems. *Plume* establishes its place on the literary scene somewhere above fashion, apart from all questions of Hipster vs. ... whatever. The work within its pages has the unpredictable, idiosyncratic strength of things that haunt, and may endure."
~ *Jeffrey Skinner*

"Always astonishing and diverse in content, *Plume* is one of our most elite and essential online journals and a roving museum of contemporary poetry curated by Daniel Lawless. 'Glancing blow' after glancing blow, it makes me hungry, ad infinitum, for the strange and beautiful—and the annual anthology is a sumptuous feast of enduring American poetry."
~ *Mark Irwin*

"Like a bird landing in the absent shadow of a bird,
Plume has gorgeously and unabashedly
taken up residence inside an inner vane, an ache
in contemporary poetry, and sunk its hooklets in.
Now many of us cannot exist without it,
so drab and songless does a world without *Plume* seem to seem...."
~ *Robin Behn*

"Like *Antaeus* and *Ironwood*, two of the greatest American poetry magazines of the past fifty years, *Plume* is eclectic in the most purposeful and pleasurable of ways. In a very short amount of time, Danny Lawless has made it a 'must-read' like no other. *Plume* is one of my favorite sources for new poetry—online or in print. Thoughtful, entertaining, capacious, with no use for aesthetic axe-grinding, its highly-enriched oxygen will add energy to your life!"
~ *David Rivard*

"Among the new magazines of recent years in print and on-line formats, one—*PLUME*—stands above all the rest and offers us both venues. What a delight it is to read the work of newcomers beside the poems of poets I've followed for years! The eclecticism of the editor's taste never ceases to amaze me. I just used the print anthology in my Advanced Poetry Writing Workshop at Tulane and the students echoed my enthusiasm.
~ *Peter Cooley*

THE PLUME ANTHOLOGY OF POETRY is a wild and lovely gathering of poems and poets. Lawless has pulled together a time and place in a selection of some of the most interesting work being done.
~ *Laura Kasischke*

Elegant *Plume* appeared with the flourish of a cyberquill pen in 2011 and quickly became the place where superlative poets showcase their brightest work. Editor Danny Lawless displays his adoration for electric, emotional and, dare I say, meaningful poetry—and for poets themselves—with all the vigor of a steward of this art. Once a year the revered, sparky, sagacious *Plume* comes into print, subtly changing our cultural foundations. Hold it, read it, and applaud!
~ *Molly Peacock*

Reading *Plume* is like having a conversation with your best friend, your best self, and all the people who love the world in its beauty and craziness.
~ *Barbara Hamby*

Preface
Daniel Tobin

Whale-song, bird-song, sea surf, wind, thunder, Bach, Beethoven, Mozart, Stravinsky, Chuck Berry, Blind Willie Johnson, Valya Balkanska, spoken greetings in fifty-five languages beginning with Akkadian, a double-helix whirl of human DNA, a newborn, children at play, a family reunion, a map of Earth, the alps, an atoll, Monument Valley, a woman raking leaves, a sequoia, the Taj Majal, the Golden Gate, a highway, a chambered nautilus, a school of dolphins, a hand: these are just a few of the sounds and images launched into space in 1977 on the golden records of Voyager 1, that legendary spacecraft with its time capsule curated by the late Carl Sagan. Though it looks like it might have been fashioned by Rube Goldberg, Voyager's this-worldly montage of where and what and who we are, pitched to the otherworldly denizens of the universe (if there are any), has by now travelled well beyond the solar system into the vastness of interstellar space. In forty thousand years, more or less, it will pass within 1.6 light years of Gliese 445 in the constellation Camelopardalis—"*Per aspera ad astra*," one of the records reads, "through adversity to the stars."

It would not be imprecise to say that poetry anthologies are also time capsules, offering a glimpse of the art in its cultural / historical moment and aspiring through the welcome adversities of publication and the hopes of readership to break free of the immediate editorial orbit, hopefully to establish for a time some gravity of their own. It is fair to say that over the past few years the Plume Anthologies have broken free in just this kind of exciting way to become—at the risk of extending the conceit boldly beyond where any preface has gone before—an attractor of exemplary poets and discriminating readers. In *The Plume Anthology of Poetry 4*, one finds as in any attentively (read, in Plume's case, remarkably) curated time capsule an extraordinarily representative variety of formal approaches and voices—lyrics, narratives, ekphrastic poems, prose poems, translations, parables, all from a range of geographies and ethnicities, poems that celebrate natural beauties, others that condemn the injustice and ugliness of human history. One finds wormholes, coronas, radiographs, Tuscan light, lightwaves, ocean waves, and bees—a great many bees accomplishing all manner of literal and metaphorical labors—swallows, deer, a gopher, a flying pig, dreams, orgasms, cathedrals, hallucinations, literary lions, ars poeticas, preludes, fugues, ghosts, and God.

With so much diversity of sensibility the risk might be cacophony, but not in Daniel Lawless's accomplished editorial hands. Like the online *Plume*, which has quickly come to be the standard for digital poetry journals, his fourth Plume anthology, like the earlier incarnations, keeps its center of gravity in the indomitably eclectic acuity of its editor. Recently, installation artist Trevor Paglen launched another time capsule into orbit around the Earth for when, billions of years into the future, the human presence has been entirely erased from the planet. Soon, another time capsule, KEO, is planned to attain its escape velocity. There will be an accelerating plume to engineer its aspiration. Once again, gratefully, we have ours here and now.

Introduction

Readers—

As you no doubt do not recall, this space was occupied last year, in *The Plume Anthology of Poetry 3*, by some remarks on the origins of the book you hold in your hands. Next year, perhaps there will be a peek into the future. For this installment, however, I want—briefly!—to annotate the present: to answer if I can an existential question, self-posed: Why is Plume here? And equally important—*still?*

Regarding the first, a glance over my shoulder is necessary. As noted in that allusion to volume 3, our journal in both its online and print iterations is the quintessential late-bloomer; its roots were planted—unknown to me at the time, of course—some forty years ago, after a trip to San Francisco, where I was entranced by the nascent punk scene, especially the band posters and promotional flyers affixed to telephone poles, mailboxes, walls, and such. Returning to Louisville, Kentucky, I followed suit, in a way, stapling my own poems and those of others I had been reading to the same public canvases. A delight, mostly, my endeavors gaining some cloistered notoriety for a while, but which came to an abrupt end when that seminal movement, heretofore absent in the heartland, finally materialized and seemingly overnight with its steady parade of local bands' promotional materials masked my publications with their own turgid blandishments. At a loss as to what to do next, as usual I retreated into a sort of high-functioning slumber, until awakening once more only many years later under the most serendipitous of circumstances—while perusing the contents of a student's computer screen. Vaguely suspicious (though more curious than caring) he might not be completely engaged in the assignment at hand, I discovered instead of scrolling through porn or perusing some turbid anarchist tract, he was instead reading poetry in the online magazine *Pank*. Shocked as if I had encountered a digital re-apparition of those old punk posters and poems, or as if apprehending in another form ye olde *Anteus* or *Ironweed*, it dawned on me that I might do this, too, and determined quickly to learn how I might put together such a magazine myself: *Plume*, as it turned out (née *Canisy*, after the town and book of the same name by Follain).

Which brings us to the other question, of its *continued* existence.

Are you thinking I refer to the impediments that have shipwrecked many another literary magazine, from, say, *Spelunker Flophouse* to the rather more sorely missed *Anderbo*? Nasty items such a lack of financial support, a less than omnipresent social media presence, wandering staff? You'd be correct, of course. But not entirely—although all of these and more might be ascribed to *Plume*. What I mean is, more precisely, how is it that *I, Danny Lawless*, am still editing *Plume*? (*I*, because after all, for good or ill, and not intending in any measure to devalue the contributions of its gifted and stellar volunteer crew, the journal remains for all intents and purposes, *la mienne*.)

Short answer: I'm not sure.

For, honestly, if the past is any guide, *Plume should* have folded long ago.

Oh, I can mumble truthfully that it was never actually meant to endure, its demise written in the code as it were. Certainly from inception it was ill-formed, with only the vague sense of a "mission" but utterly bereft of the slightest notion of professionalism, let alone a recognizable business plan, the idea of which I would have found as perplexing as it was laughable; undertaken mostly as a lark, a whim, little more than a distraction from all I needed distracting from then, primarily the crushing boredom that shadows any activity that has become rote, in my case teaching. An *exercise in reverie* if you will, of the cinematic sort: watch the formerly vaunted high school point guard (though I was never so vaulted!) resurrect his eroded skills in a pick-up game at the Y with opponents half his age, or the retired executive—shudder—teach those whiz kids a thing or two in the start-up boardroom. (I think this was an actual film.)

But I think the real reason *Plume should* have gone the way of those other publishing endeavors, in the end is not at all attributable to the circumstances common to all such ventures in the digital era, mentioned above. Nor even its inauspicious *raison d'être*. No, that it *should* have failed is due entirely to my own character. For contrary to our imagined film-ic heroes, I am not by nature one who *in practice* actually tries anything, tests himself. Rather the opposite: in in my soul, high and wide, I am instead that most bathetic of creatures: a runaway. A reflexive if miniaturized Bartleby. A shirker, a goldbrick, a layabout.

It began early, this tendency to demur, turn heel whenever confronted with, let's face it, anything that smacked of work, commitment, diligence. (I know, Bartleby had other things on his mind.)

How clearly the words of countless teachers and well-meaning would-be bosses and mentors over the years ring in my ears even now, like a premature spoken epitaph: "if only he applied himself."

The phrase initially was launched probably by my first grade instructor in yet another parent-teacher conference. Like some of you, I attended a parochial elementary school. And as most in those halcyon years—1960–1968—mine, Saint Raphael's, was located in my own neighborhood. In fact, from that first grade classroom's windows, I could see our house—*my* house. And see it I did, that first-day-of-school sweltering August morning: no, not see, but gazed fixedly upon it as with X-ray vision, as the forbidding Sister Angelina attempted to ensconce us in our assigned seats and began her fantastical recitation of the myriad rules by which we were to be governed. Immediately I knew: there was nothing for it but to flee. By reason of those incomprehensible regulations, yes, but much more important because of what I believed I could spy *à la* the Man of Steel transpiring within the red brick walls of 2826 Eleanor Avenue: my mother, caught in a most egregious act of betrayal—preparing a breakfast of sugar-crusted cinnamon toast and crisp bacon for my three-year-old brother as she only the day before had prepared it for *me*. In other words: I had been replaced. It could not stand. So, waiting until our habited overseer was distracted by something or other, I slipped between the desks and skittered out the door, making tracks to the familial manse with the intention of confronting the two. Which I did, and was met by a disappointingly gentle if earnest rebuke, and promptly escorted hand-in-hand by the principal traitor, along with the smirking, toddling object of my disaffection, to my proper place, making my re-entrance amid the suppressed cackles of what obviously had been mislabeled my "new friends." And though this sibling jealousy abated in the ensuing weeks and months, the habit of running away did not. Instead, I took to squirming free from that Catholic fortress as instinctively as children everywhere the perfumed embrace of a rickety aunt, and at every opportunity—on the way to morning Mass, in line for restroom breaks. To do what? Not much. Wander the surrounding neighborhoods and later those farther-flung, dodging unrestrained dogs and dawdling in drainage ditches, crossing busy streets to reach the Key Market to procure with my lunch money the sustenance necessary to continue my peregrinations, in the form of licorice strings or Milky Way bars, and chocolate milk. Each time, of course, I was eventually intercepted by a vigilant housewife or yard-worker, occasionally one or another volunteer from the teams of engineers from General Electric who were my father's colleagues, glad for their own chance to temporarily abscond from *their* duties, whatever they were. Until, finally, I found myself hog-tied with sturdy rope to my school desk by the otherwise kindly janitor, where I remained for a good number of weeks longer, capitulating only upon receiving the heady promise of being permitted, each morning, to refill the holy water stations that adorned every threshold door throughout the school, thus shaving a good forty-five minutes off my educational day, not to mention the prestige of the position itself, normally reserved for an upper-classman.

I did say I would be brief, didn't I? Sorry.

So I will be, then. Stopping only for a moment to admire the view from the I-65 South on-ramp, where at fourteen I perched on a duffel bag like my friend Mike Edsall, our thumbs stuck out with the studied casualness we had admired in older travelers; en route to Miami, and thence to Jamaica, with the ingenious plan to purchase hashish (with funds not from lunch money this time but in my case collected from my trusting paper route customers) at a considerable discount from a few no doubt good-hearted local Rasta's and return to distribute to our 9ᵗʰ grade colleagues at the public school we attended. An adventure that ended badly, needless to say—juvenile detention in Miami Beach, a silent plane ride home to Louisville in the care of a large policeman. Still, *fun* and *weird* in every permutation of those words, for the week or so of our absence, with the delayed recompense too that the (imagined) particulars of our hiatus had been broadcast via the usual gossips, and assumed the proportions of myth: even seniors treated us like gods.

After that, the regular progression of the inveterate runaway (or freshly minted "slacker"): fleeing now from employment, now college, from relationships, from god forbid! concerns about insurance or health care of all things, and kids. Drifting, to be kind. Through Europe and ever-smaller and more dilapidated apartments, through books and more books, through the first years of my marriage and all the semesters of my so-called teaching career. A spectral version of myself, ventriloquizing inwardly as every adolescent of whatever age must, the state if not the actual words of my idol Cioran, from *De l'inconvénient d'être né*:

"The same feeling of not belonging, of futility, wherever I go: I pretend interest in what matters nothing to me, I bestir myself mechanically or out of charity, without ever being caught up, without ever being somewhere. What attracts me is elsewhere, and I don't know where that elsewhere is."

Until arriving at that epiphanic moment in a Creative Writing class in 2012, where this note began.

So the backstory. But why have I stuck with it, these four-plus years? I said I wasn't sure, though I can venture a hypothesis: because it felt good. Really? I hear you say. Yes. Nothing more. And what more is needed? For I had accidentally discovered my ... self. One that I never knew existed. And of all places—in work! Steadiness! Wretched stick-to-it-iveness! That dread thing which had pursued me and from which I had so long recoiled as naturally as at the thought of incest or the extended company of Pete Rose. From that moment on, until this one, as I write, I could and can at last say I understood Conrad's line from *Heart of Darkness*:

"I don't like work—no man does—but I like what is in the work—the chance to find yourself. Your own reality—for yourself not for others—what no other man can ever know."

From Cioran to Conrad—two very different figures and quite a distance.

Yet I *have* found myself—whatever self there is to find, if the self exists at all—a discussion for another forum. In any event I *believe* that I have, and this sensation is one that is essentially a form of faith, isn't it? Nor will you be surprised when I say that it was there along, this crouching ineffable self, invisibly accompanying me in those seemingly wasted years, when as if "out of these scattered things,/something serious and lasting were being planned."

"Serious and lasting"? I hope so, but don't count on it. And what is this Thing, anyway, with its also Rilke-ean capital, so transformative that, were it with the mind or the heart that we apprehended others, not the body, I would appear to my closest allies unrecognizable? Put simply, it is the opportunity *Plume* has given me to take *my life* seriously, to discover in its work something of value, which, though you might have your own reservations about just what that value might comprise, has been, can I say revelatory—no, fascinating? A capacious word, that one. From *fascinus*, "to bring under a spell, as by the power of the eye." Yet where else can I locate the … joy that overtakes me when I find in my Inbox or in Submittable a poem by a master such as Linda Bierds or Tom Sleigh, Major Jackson, Beckian Goldberg or Daniel Tobin or D. Nurkse? Do I open the attachment with the avidity of the collector his mailed specimen, the beaded brow of the super-fan or Nabokov-ian suitor? I do. Well, not quite that, but not *wholly* dissimilar either. See me there, at my desk, ensorcelled as the Florida night-breeze outside my office window lays its hand on the cheek of the rescued alley cat at my feet, who purrs at its touch, or as on some nameless square out of Calvino entices spectral men again to their ancient duels—the ceaseless clatter of palm fronds. See me as I see my own face dimly reflected in the screen before me, a ghostly figure wandering—again—though not through neighborhoods though neighborhoods in a way—but among the lines unfolding before my eyes, be they Ellen Bass's "… Bit of breath/I bury under a stone./Scruffy soul, unlucky/scribble of life …" or Carl Phillips' "… somewhere/grace, too, lies hidden. Nobody/speaks to me as you do. Nowhere/water-lit do the leaves pale faster." Or others, so many. Hours slink by. Another escape hatch, sure, this reading. But one through which I pass safely, unchecked, un-searched for, into a world of the most breathtaking beauty and unspeakable horrors. In that there *is* a life, I now know.

Fascination bifurcated, too, I ought to say—since alongside this fascination with the work itself, I find as an editor I am invested with the vicarious power of casting that spell on others: you, dear readers, who will find *your* selves in these poems, perhaps, understand their magic, allow for their petty grievances sometimes and join in their majestic lamentations. Another delight. A shaman, then? Hardly. Barely a conduit—one that remains largely undiscovered, too. And that's OK. For much as I wish I could claim I do it for you, I don't. You—passers-by on these pages—rarely intrude on my private reveries, certainly have no say in which ones I choose to share, which direction they shall take. And yet here we are. You have found me, and I, you. Readers of Plume— you whom I barely know. That you are reading these words astonishes me. Almost as much as the inexplicable grace with which you—and you, too, poets, most of all—have treated me, this former runaway (but unreconstructed goldbrick and lay about, I'm afraid). The sensed shelter of your *presence*, you must know, means everything.

Daniel Lawless
Editor, *Plume*
16 January 2016

Contents

Two Blessings
~ Ekiwah Adler-Beléndez

I thought being in a wheelchair
was the same thing as being useless

so I demanded for the women I loved
to dress me, cook for me, shower me
and put on my shoes every morning.

I thought having stiff legs meant
having stiff hands a stiff brain
and a flaccid cock.

Even when I made love fully undressed
I was afraid of my skin. I saw it as a vortex
I could float in forever. We never quite managed
to make love naked.

It was only when one woman left me
that I began to learn
out of determination and grief

the marvels of the hand held shower,
or the way a broken egg sunny side up
is a rapidly expanding planet
that is bright at the center

or the difference between
a right and a left shoe
and that small buttons
are an odyssey for my fingers
better solved with Velcro.

I began to learn how real desire
takes root in the body
and extends beyond it

how love is blessing when it comes
and blessing too—when it leaves.

Waltz of the Orbital Decay in Our Relationship
~ Kelli Russell Agodon

Some days, we feel like specks.
    Some days there's a strange
    breath between us,

and you're dripping ink on my palm,
    talking to me about baptism.
    Tell me again how ghost satellites

are everywhere. Tell me
    how we become the swirl
    of ink to make a poem.

You say the universe is enormous, beyond
    enormous and you imagine constellations
    in the shapes of saxophones,

though I'm not sure how the universe
    has a solo, why jazz makes me undress.
    I'm not sure why the sound of rain

on the roof reminds me of dying
    and sometimes seeing the sky
    makes me feel alone.

Some nights I'm not enough
    for anyone. Some nights
    the moon is a hand across my body,

a mouth across my thigh. We say want
    to be more than Damian Peach's
    supernova, but we want to be part of it,

the peach tree in a field of stars
  —the wind, the clouds, the being.
  You are my devoted satellite

and sometimes I capture you
  thoughtlessly, while many times,
  I am the scientist who sends you away.

أنظر إليك
مرام المصري

18

انسلت
بين الأغطية
قطعت أنفاسها
مختبئة في أبعد زوايا السرير

حلقة قرطي
وحدها
التي كادت
تنجو

32

حسبتها
خطواتك
دقات
قلبي
المتلاحقة

35

لا
ليس بابك
الذي أطرق
والذي
اسمع
خلفه
انفاسها
والذي
رغم انكسار مصراعيه
لا يفتح

from *I Look at You*
Maram Al-Masri, translated by Hélène Cardona

18

In the corner of the bed, hidden
she holds her breath …
and sneaks
between the covers.

Alone,
alone, my earring
almost survived.

32

I took them
for your steps
the palpitations
of my heart …

35

No, it's not on your door
that I knock,
the door behind which
I hear
breathing
the door
broken off its hinges
which still refuses
to open.

Granadas
~ Sandra Alcosser

> *Holy week of lace, of canaries flying amid the tapers,*
> *of an air that was lukewarm and sad.*
> —Federico Garcia Lorca

Pretending to filch from a branch
He wrapped an airy globe with his hand
Poured liqueur into its split hide
Sucked between his teeth, closed his eyes

La Doña I asked as though his mother might
Have made this drink Saturday nights
When Salvador his father was alive
La Doña I asked again and her son frightened

La Doña in a pink sand castle
With her shack of sons behind laughing
While she napped—rancheros
On the radio and pool games
Under the wooden lath
That mothered their tangle of hanging plants

NIGHT-BLOOMING CEREUS

The month of the crawl space
The attic before winter rains
La Doña's son arrived
With wrenches hacksaw pliers
Plumber's tools in a tombstone case
To ruch up then sweep our drains
And after a few hours I paid him grateful
For his silent labor

Invisible as dusk he stood by my gate—
Hinges straining—
Pulled out shims drivers straightened
Gravity's weight then bowed and smiled at me
Granadas he said waving
His hands at the pomegranate tree

BESIDE THE FIRETHORN

As if the mention of his mother's name sobered
Him—widow who'd never spoken
To me or waved as her boys walked her slowly
Under the shade awning bathing her in roses
Of unnatural coral unnatural as though
Nowhere in the world were petals so
Thick or fragrant or deep in color
As the roses of *La Doña* and Salvador

Triste the son asked and I did not know
If he spoke of himself or *La Doña*
Or perhaps of me three
Figures snugged into bungalows
Above the sea *No not sad* I said making
A skirt of my t-shirt to fill with pomegranates

Tiny Side-Blotched Lizards Grow Less Timid

Too sexual—blooming
Since April each bud grew
Like lipstick rising from a tube
Pomegranates tasting of human
Flesh spun like planets—
Mars of burnished leather—splattered
On concrete rolled into the grass
Solo he said and I answered *no no solo*

Uncertain whether he asked if I lived alone
Or was I lonely unable to speak the same
Or understand anything but hands I made
A basket and waved him out the gate
And we became two white
Shirts tacking *solo* into night

UNDER THE FLAME TREE

You may sip the flesh swallow the seeds
But there are always too many
Waiting in pulpy chambers
Like secrets the way we mistake
A gesture *No no solo* I'd said *Take*
The granadas I could not stop placing
More in his basket and though
We lived as neighbors years after *La Doña*

Died and her pink castle sat empty
I could only imagine her son's shame
When I lied *nunca triste nunca solo*
Holy as a god *never sad never lonely*
As if one could ever be
More than a human body

Hard Dreaming
~ Meena Alexander

Dear mother, grandmother died with absolutely no warning
Left you a raw girl clad in cotton,
Barely sixteen, weeping into your own sleeve.
No mother and a father who did not really care for you—
Forced to walk on eggshells

Rub a dub dub of wretched want and need,
Stony tutelage.

In grandmother's diary, a firm rounded hand,
The recipe for mutton curry
Squats next to Gandhi's injunctions to spin.
Grandmother wonders what to pay the dhobi,
The woman who pounds rice
The man who harvests pepper
From the twisted vines in the garden.

Must she burn all her silks in the nationalist bonfire,
Can she keep a few?

I have laid out my khadi, washed and ironed it.
Tomorrow when I wear it, the sky will be blue.

Far to the north
In the half-timbered stables where I lodge
I listen for the snort of horses
Crude rub of saddle against flank,
Englishmen with polished boots
Yelling for valet, butler, chowkidar.

When hailstones strike the roof
I shove grandmother's diaries into a leather suitcase
Under my bed. Later I crouch on the floor
With buckets under all the spots
Where the ceiling darkens and water drips.

Charred whispers scarcely audible
The centuries doubling back, feverish, irresolute—

Children bearing firewood
For the fretted furnaces of lords and ladies,
White haired women with their makeshift canes
Bodies bent in a hoarse wind
That rattles bridge and bay window
Spews dirt onto pillar and polished marble
The furious wealth of empire.

Then quick hooves of horses in caracole
Forcing me to shut my eyes and dream—
Hard dreaming, mother, on a cold mountain slope.

Children from a little school
Beat drums, chant their lessons.
What do they learn?

A brown bird cries out from the deodar trees.
It has no name.
It makes warbling cries I cannot catch.

Nothing to punctuate those sounds
Except wild air.

The heart's illiterate, Dear Mother
No reading or writing in those bloody clavicles.

Only whispered words, illegible sentences
And all the marks the body bears
Violent, ecstatic, lingering.

Why I Am Not an Orgasm
~ Nin Andrews

after Frank O'Hara

I am not an orgasm. I'm a poet.
Why? I think I'd rather be
an orgasm. But I'm not. Well,

not today. My husband is
in bed, reading the news.
When I bend to kiss him, he says,
"Lie down, why don't you?" And
I do. The orgasm does, too, or it
thinks about it. Together we
slide between the sheets.

"You're still reading the news," I say.
"Yes," my husband says and absently
pats my arm. "What's happening?"
I ask. "Bibi Netanyahu won
the election," he says.
That's when the orgasm leaves.
It doesn't care for Bibi Netanyahu.
Neither does my husband.

I feel so lonesome then, so bereft.
I walk to the desk and begin to type
random words. They undulate in slow
waves through my mind. They do not tell
the truth. They say I live in a city
of dust and crows. I'm the most beautiful
red-head alive. Today, wearing a pink
satin blouse, I stretch out beneath the palm

trees to warm my nut-brown thighs. I
stop writing. Outside it's beginning to rain.
I sip weak coffee and give the dog
a biscuit. I call the poem, "Orgasm,"
even if there is not a single orgasm
in that dusty Texas town.

Song of the Orgasm
~ Nin Andrews
after Whitman

Every atom of me belonging to me belongs to you, and you know it, you who loaf so freely about my soul, and have for eons, you, as lean as a spear of meadow grass, a stalk of wheat, always I see you, and everywhere

even here, when you are a thousand miles away (for Christ's sake, love, when will you be back? So much time has passed since I last touched your face, and still I dream, I wait), I can't help but breathe you in, your scent in every room in me, in every corner and shelf, in each moment I inhale, intoxicant that you are, illegal substance ... you, I should not let you, not now, not ever, not you

who are on my lips, tongue, fingers, hair, forever I taste the fragrance of you. I am so in love with it, I will go to the brink of my mind, exposed, nude, mad to be in contact with you ...

Burning
~ Ralph Angel

The mind *is* the plot, it goes
where it goes. My house, its loneliness, page

after page the moon dies in the sun, the sun
scatters the stars.

Sometimes I think I'm in the mail. And
burn them.

"A crow takes off
above our heads and sinks

into the scattered
thoughts of a wandering cloud."

It's in your eyes, the way you walk, your
swiftness.

Feeling Today
~ Rae Armantrout

Could it be
the problem of
modern reflexology
is to keep tongue in cheek
while cultivating
melancholy
in the red-shifted context
of the retro surreal?

*

Oh,
pale pink ballpoint
with ADVENTURE IMAGING
stamped on your carapace
in letters that mimic
a message
dug in wet sand
with a stick
by a cast-away
on a sound stage
in the late
1950s,
you could almost
but not quite
mean what we
feel

A Few Questions
~ Rae Armantrout

Is it that a pocket
enjoys being filled

or that the folds
want to be pushed

aside
because they're tired

of touching
one another?

*

What if my sex
fantasies don't
involve me,

but rather
two strangers?

*

As I rock,
the dazzle

on the glass lid
splits, the top

half turns red
crested, then subsides

into itself
again.

(To make this happen
feels like happiness.)

    *

When the disc dissolves,
have I solved
for X?

A Trespass
~ Simon Armitage

On the raw shoulder
    of Royd Edge, the upper limb
        of a storm-snapped beech

has ended up wedged
    on a lower branch.
        A little finger

will easily rock
    that two-pronged bough
        in the tree's crook,

but no amount
    of deranged swinging
        can hope to unhook

the dead from the living.
    The winds of the world
        blast and rattle

that private wood,
    and the wishbone rides
        in the tuning fork.

Plate 41   Death Figure
~ Sally Ball

[a photograph by Linda Connor]

He waits, alert, chalked on a brick wall.
(Exterior?) Above him in the eaves
hovers a row of masks, hovering there as if to quell
whatever might think to rise: they alternate,
a skull, a man, a skull, an angry man …

The faces darker or lighter, bearded or not,
at peace or in pain, enraged—it depends.
But the skulls all struggle to stay wrapped
around the void. *Do not pull us loose,*
they fairly seethe—

So on the wall, below those death's heads,
reaching one hand up in their direction,
the chalked man floats. Not frail; ethereal.
His outline darker than the wash
of white that fills him.

You know he's flesh (not only bones)
because his penis matters, his form
is swathed as if in ligaments.
He might be dancing, Travolta-like,
or steadying himself, to keep from falling backward.

The carved stone abutments seem less real,
more merely referential,
than this featherweight,
who owns the photograph,
which someone *made.* Though human hands

23

and human will made every element of what we see:
the wall, the masks, the ornament, the frame
through which we see it now, composed.
Inside of which he, this chalked-up figure, alters
the apparent heft

and actual meaning of the stones—
even as they constitute the wall,
a very old wall, I'm sure.
Emaciated, yet strong, he has
an elegance. Like a ghost,

he disappears into, emerges from
the wall. Like a ghost's, the lightness of his touch
annuls the wall. He must be gone now,
rained off or worn or washed away.
Right here, this photograph

is where he lives, all his strength accrues
from you, from us—from being seen.

Plate 41   Death Figure 2
~ Sally Ball

Additional details: sharp intrusion,
a chalked spear or dagger,
pointed at the chalked man's abs,

also a spot of birdshit,
right below the single poised statue of a bird—
which looks ready to take wing—

Is the excrement left by the kind of bird
who really flies and eats and shits,
or is it also chalk? Har, har.

And interspersed between the aggressions
of the masks: stone-carved moon and sun,
intricate flowers and leaves,

each human grimace undergirded
by a bloom,
a light.

Visser, 50 v. Chr.
~ Benno Barnard

Wat deed ik anders aan de rivier
dan fuiken uitzetten, luisteren naar oude
bloeddoorlopen verhalen, grommende
in haar binnendringen en een gouden
zoon voor na mij maken?

Goed, dat was vroeger.
Maar het was deze oever, waar het gebeurde
dat ik bij maanlicht, onder het knopen
van netten, tegen het bosrijke donker daarginder
iets wonderlijks mompelde,

iets dat ik zelf niet begreep –
over een roerdomp bijvoorbeeld, en niet over helden.
Wat was het? Waar kwam het vandaan? En waarom
zocht het mijn mond, de mond van een man
in een simpele boot

op de Schelde?
Ik luisterde naar onze exegeten, maa zonder te weten
of ze de drassige aarde wel konden verklaren.
Ik geloofde nooit dat we ooit kathedralen en zo
zouden gaan bouwen.

Begrijpt u me rustig verkeerd.
In een bocht van de grote rivier
heb ik een zoon mogen maken
en hem in het dampende zonlicht der vroegte
mijn knopen geleerd.

Fisherman, 50 BC
~ Benno Barnard, translated by David Colmer

What else would I do on the river
but set my nets and listen to old
blood-drenched stories, growl as I
penetrate her and make a golden
son for when I'm gone?

Fine, that was then.
But on this bank it happened,
that I, by moonlight, while mending
nets, mumbled something strange
to the forest of darkness opposite,

something that baffled even me—
about a bittern, for instance, and not some great Celt.
What was it? Where did it come from? And why
did it seek my mouth, the mouth of a man
in a simple boat

on the Scheldt?
I listened to our sages, not knowing
if they could explain the marshy earth,
never believing that one day we
would build cathedrals and such.

Feel free to get me wrong.
In a bend of a mighty river
I got to make a son
and in the steaming light of dawn
I taught him my knots.

Elegy for a Gopher
~ Ellen Bass

The pads of your paws scrabble
as I drag you from the tunnel
clamped to the shiny green trap,
a baby, hell-bent on saving
your twist of life, spun
from the same cells as I am, the common
intelligence of fins, wings, limbs.
The first time you see the sun
you're splayed on your back, the shadow
of my blade above you.
Your ears, tiny colorless petals,
and at the tips of your articulated fingers,
ten frantic claws. When I strike,
your mouth opens stunningly
wide, a scream so silent
all sound is sucked down the naked
whirlpool of your throat. I hate
that I can salvage nothing.
I can't skin and eat you, stuff or display
your fur on the mantel.
I won't carve a needle
from your bone. Bit of breath
I bury under a stone.
Scruffy soul, unlucky
scribble of life, guilty of nothing.

The Parable of the Car
~ Charles Baxter

In the dream-parable of the car
I am behind the wheel of one
of the many unreliable sedans
that I have owned, some now so
obscure they are unheard of by
younger generations—for example
my first, the Simca 1000, engine
in the back and transverse mounted,
or the Fiat 128, now *there* was a real
lemon, with the spare tire stored on
the engine block, the entire
machine being counter to good
sense and intuition,
and that thing was preceded
by the AMCs, a Javelin
and then a Pacer, clown car
and laughingstock, and of course
the dull Dodge Shadow and The Boat,
a giant Chevrolet; and in the dream

I am myself, and as myself
I turn the key,
and it turns over once
and starts, whereupon I am
astonished, so I put the car in gear
and suddenly we are on the highway,
and what I feel is joy, the most serious
and rare, and every year I dream
myself into that junker place
staring through the windshield
at what's coming, and I am taken there

29

by something that is broken,
smashed, rusted, already in
oblivion, mal-designed, wrecked,
crushed, scattered in a thousand
junkyards, dead and unresurrected—
but, sweet jesus, it starts, it runs.

Garden Path Project
~ Robin Behn

Starting out on the garden path
project nothing; be the sun being
the lace the light is making
of your face, a path in a shape that shapes
your going, the whole of what warms you
making your way now for
this is the day for it day has been
approaching, your day, daystar,
little blazing meaning
on your forehead like the star
on the horse's forehead that horses
the horse forward, riding
in your mind, that started out still still
but out, and, starting, yes, upon
the ground, the ground
the light ate none of
that goes, here, to ground for you,
the horse of you, blazing, it is
Little Star, your day!

    Time, you walk on by.
    Heraldry, shine.
    Manic, be lyric.
    Garden, be mine.

Liliya in Omchak
~ April Bernard

1.
Late winter, and I
was such a little girl
when the wolves, the last
seen in those parts,
came into the town,
prowling, mad for food.
A long grey tongue
drooped over red gums
and frothy teeth shone
as one hugely nosed,
panting, into our garden:
It looked straight at me
through the window and I
was too scared to scream.
The men were gone on a hunt;
Aunt Magda got the rifle
and shot them, first
the one at our steps,
blew away its face;
then the other, running
and limping down the street
past the train tracks.
I could scream then.

2.

The blasted wolf-face
was wet and gray and white
and tangly spilling red.
The boys ran and kicked
its head like a ball, shouting.
We built a fire from scrap
wood and logs we stole
from Old Peter's pile.
We burned the wolves
and did not think until later
we had burned good meat.
Our mothers never even
tried to stop us.

3.

Even the lingonberries were gone
and we had eaten both
the ponies by the time
the men returned from the hunt
with nothing. So they drank.
The story of meaty wolves
wasted in their absence
filled them with rage.
My oldest brother, bigger
already than our father,
pushed Aunt Magda
down the cellar stairs
and broke her jaw. We hid
in corners the long weeks
until spring. Then the fish
ran again in the river
and the western railroad
returned with food in cans
and flour and salt and seeds
for planting. The men hitched
themselves to the plows and we
were needed in the fields to steer
and to hoe, very careful
for always until now, here,
about which stories to tell.

Confederate Battle Flag
~ Charles Bernstein

Selling loose cigarettes
Changing lanes in duress
Aren't warrant for arrest
Much less sudden death

Color: An Elegy
~ Linda Bierds

The yellow reflected by the bee's thorax
and scientist's sleeve, by the gold-topped glint
of seven entomology pins, no longer exists,
its formula—lead-tin, fire, the binder's precise
environment—lost.
            And the mineral green
of the shallow spoon at the bee's tongue-tip, exists
but is gone: too much heat or chill or the complex
erosions of light.
            Almost gone but fully there,
the semi-transparent, outstretched wing
is as finely leaded at the room's distant window,
painted in shaky perspective
but offering, with the wing, a brush stroke
of philosophical symmetry: how thin the membranes
that free us from the world.
            Although the world
of 1637, its gradually rising tinted ground,
has climbed through the huge, anatomical bee,
the hind legs and faded pollen basket,
has climbed through the pins
and window, which is, in fact,
                    outside the frame
but bright on the curve of the bee's black eye.
There, and also there, the silk-sleeved figure
of Song Yingxing once bent in reflection
across the panes. That is our earth, he said,
stopped in the prism
            of an insect's eye:
catties of copper, wagons of loam, bronze hives
like lamps on the cliffsides. And the five

enduring grains, the greens, the reds,
the ungreenable whites—
                              This is beauty's way,
isn't it? Song once said: on the finite curve
of a bee's dark eye, all that light can carry
across a harrowed land.

We Were Our Father's Second Family
~ Sally Bliumis-Dunn

Bright rectangles on the living-room wall
where the pictures must have hung,
we slept in their old rooms,

a black cast-iron hitching post
though we owned no horses; round white
millstones like giant moons held down
in the overgrown grass.

Father's past in our present—
sometimes we'd sense it poking through
the gravelly chop of his voice—
the tall grass bending in the fields

bent toward it, the shadows
beneath the blades.

La Promenade en Fôret
~ Yves Bonnefoy

Cher Christian, vous souvenez-vous de cette longue promenade que nous avons faite en forêt d'Ardenne ? En quelle année c'était, ne nous le demandons pas.

Nous étions partis de Charleville où vous étiez venu nous rejoindre, Lucy et moi, dans votre petite voiture. Il pleuvait un peu, comme nous quittions la ville. Mais bientôt ce fut un faible soleil.

La veille nous avions revu la tombe, la statue. Mais était-ce bien ce que nous cherchions ? Non, la tombe de cet ami que nous avons eu, vous et moi, cette tombe est transparente, c'est de l'air, c'est une nuée arrêtée au dessus d'un de nos chemins.

Et nous voici dans la grande forêt maintenant. Avec ses longues voies qui frôlent parfois, n'est-ce qu'un faux souvenir, des échancrures béantes dans des falaises : et là le ciel est plus vaste. Nous avons ramassé des éclats d'ardoise. J'imaginais qu'Ubac nous accompagnait, silencieux comme si souvent.

Lui que j'avais vu enduire de peinture bleue ou ocre rouge ou vert sombre d'autres de ces débris de la pierre grise avant de les presser sur de grandes feuilles. C'était pour un livre où il y avait aussi des tombes, et quelques voix à se faire entendre au dessus d'elles. J'en écoutais le murmure dans les feuilles sèches d'un autre été qui restaient à noircir sur notre chemin.

Il y eut ce déjeuner à Rocroi.

Et vous souvenez-vous de cette rencontre que nous fîmes, l'après-midi ? Vers la fin, quand la lumière dans la forêt semble maintenant ne venir que de presque le ras du sol, là-bas, derrière les arbres ?

Trois personnes, qui venaient de là, justement. On dirait qu'elles nous ont aperçus, elles aussi, car elles se sont arrêtées, nous les voyons qui se parlent. Deux hommes, une femme ? Nous-mêmes nous voici à ne plus bouger, comme si une bête était là, toute proche de nous dans un buisson, oreilles dressées, prête à fuir. Que me dites-vous, Christian? Que me montrez-vous dans les feuilles humides de sous nos pieds ou, je ne sais plus, au creux de votre main précautionneusement refermée ? Mais à nouveau nous sommes en marche. Et eux aussi, là-bas, non, moins là-bas que déjà bien près d'ici où nous sommes. Nous allons nous croiser, sur l'unique chemin. Nous saluer, au passage.

Une femme, deux hommes, plus grands d'instants en instants sur ce fond clair de ciel de dessous sous les arbres. Et ourlés de cette lumière, si bien qu'au sein de leur forme, que c'est noir ! J'ai même cru un moment qu'ils n'avaient pas de visages, rien sur leurs épaules qu'une torche de flamme sombre trouée par instants de reflets rouges. Tout de même, ils approchent, nous les voyons mieux, ils sont … Mais c'est nous !

C'est nous, ces trois qui avancent, silencieux, bien qu'avec des sortes de petits rires. Cette femme, mais c'est toi, mon amie, sauf qu'avec un chapeau que je ne t'ai jamais vu. Une longue traînée de brume à onduler au dessus d'un col de fourrure bleu, avec des ombres de plumes. Et que tiens-tu dans tes mains ?

Et est-ce vous, Christian ? Oui, c'est vous, je ne puis vous distinguer de celui qui tout près de moi va si courageusement vers ces autres, mais qu'est-ce donc que vous teniez, et portez encore ? Est-ce un petit panier, un livre, une bête morte, non, endormie ? Mais cette fumée, tout autour ? Cette couleur qui change le ciel ? Je n'ai pas le temps de comprendre.

Car, est-ce moi ? Ce troisième, un peu en retard sur les deux autres ? Cette ombre qui porte quoi ? J'en détourne aussitôt mes yeux.

Ils sont là, près de nous, ils passent. D'un geste, à voix basse, nous nous saluons, pourrait-on faire autrement ?

Et avons-nous pensé à nous arrêter, y ont-ils songé eux aussi ? Y a-t-il eu des regards pour se croiser, des visages pour s'immobiliser un instant à la vue d'un autre semblable, des mains pour se porter en avant, visages, mains, effrayés, riants, tout à l'étonnement d'être, de n'être pas, la forêt là-haut et partout se faisant plus sombre, un dernier oiseau s'envolant au dessus de cette rencontre avec un cri de regret ? Non, je ne saurai pas ce que vous aviez entre les mains, mes amis. Et ce qu'ils portaient, ces autres. Non, nous continuons, eux et nous, sur ce chemin qui heureusement a tout de même été à cet endroit un peu large.

The Walk in the Forest
~ Yves Bonnefoy, translated by Hoyt Rogers

Dear Christian, do you remember that long walk we took in the forest in Ardenne ? What year it was, let's not ask.

We had started out from Charleville, where you'd come to join us, Lucy and me, in your little car. It was raining a bit as we left the city. But soon there was a feeble sun.

The evening before we had seen the tomb again, the statue. But was that really what we were looking for? No, the tomb of our friend, yours and mine, that tomb is transparent: it's made of air, it's a cloud standing still above one of our paths.

And here we are in the great forest now. With its long roads that sometimes—or is this only a false remembrance?—skirt gaping crevices in the cliffs: and there the sky is vaster. We gathered shards of slate. I imagined that Ubac was accompanying us, silent as so often.

I had seen him coat other fragments of the gray stone with blue, or red-ochre, or dark-green paint, before pressing them on large sheets. It was for a book that also harbored tombs—and above them, some voices made themselves heard. I listened to their murmur in the dry leaves of another summer, still remaining to blacken on our path.

There was that lunch at Rocroi.

And do you remember that encounter we had in the afternoon? Towards the end, when the light in the forest seems to come from almost flush with the ground, over there behind the trees?

Three people, who came from there, as a matter of a fact. They seemed to have caught sight of us, they as well, since we see them talking to each other. Two men, a woman? We ourselves stopped moving anymore, as if an animal were there, quite close to us in a bush, ears pricked and ready to flee. What do you tell me, Christian? What do you show me in the damp leaves under our feet, or—I no longer recall—in the palm of your hand gingerly closed? But now we're underway again. And they also, over there—no, less over there than already quite close to here where we are. We're going to join each other on the only path. Greet each other, passing by.

A woman, two men, bigger moment by moment on this glowing background of the lower sky beneath the trees. And haloed by this light, even though the core of their outline is so black ... I even thought for an instant they had no faces, nothing on their shoulders but a torch of dark flame, pierced now and then by red reflections. All the same, they come nearer, we see them better, they're ... Wait, they're us!

They're us, these three who move forward—silently, though chuckling somewhat as well. This woman—she's you, my friend, except with a hat I've never seen you wear before. A long trail of mist undulates above a brim of blue fur, with shadows of plumes. And what do you have in your hands?

And is that you, Christian? Yes, it's you. I can't distinguish you from the one who walks right next to me towards these others, so bravely. But again, what is it your were holding, and carry still? Is it a little basket, a book, a dead animal, or rather asleep? And this smoke, all around? This color that changes the sky? I don't have time to understand.

Because, is that me? This third one, lagging behind the two others a bit? This shadow who carries what? I turn my eyes from him right away.

They're there, near us; they pass by. With a gesture, in low voices, we greet each other—could we do otherwise?

And did we think of stopping, and did they consider it too? Did gazes cross, did faces freeze for a moment on seeing someone similar? Were hands held up? Faces, hands, frightened, laughing, quite astonished at being, not being, the forest up there and everywhere becoming darker, a last bird flying away above this meeting with a cry of regret? No, I will not know what you had in your hands, my friends. And what they carried, these others. No, we continue, they and we, on this path which happily, all the same, was in this place a bit wide.

Six Tuscan Poets
~ Marianne Boruch

—at the Minneapolis Institute of Art

Only three I'll remember.
Because Dante's arm sweeps across the painting's
middle distance of globe, pen,
a sextant on the table.
Because Petrarch's lovesick. Because Boccaccio
is Chaucer on steroids, his misfits
outrunning the plague's dark joke, each stab
of walking stick. *We are all*

pilgrims and strangers. So goes the stone of one
sad sweet German in Rome's
Protestant Cemetery: goodbye Hamburg, your more
bridges than Venice. For that matter, goodbye
my dear dank diseased London, Keats surely called out
over whatever fish in the sea, the ship enroute
to get him better in Rome. Dumb idea. He landed
in that graveyard face-up soon enough.
TB. Only for the best of them. Nineteenth century,
I hate you sometimes.

How these Tuscan poets still
talk to each other! Whatever year. 1575 plus now
equals on-going. In Vasari's great painting
they point to make a point,
take it down and across. Dante's emphatic—
it's Virgil he holds up
with his other beautiful hand. Petrarch fights
a word in. His pal Boccaccio above them, second tier,
looks sideways and off, destined

for the best neighborhood in my house, volume 4,
the 1910 *Britannica* which
loves the Black Death
and dreams his fleeing donkey carts.

Certain days I close my eyes and it's
our seawash, the future looking back at our
little inky spot of watery life-forms
and bad light. Then I think of something else.

Like these three, miraculous and unstuck
in the same room with me.

Cathedrals
~ David Bottoms

1

Near nightfall, in summer, an owl would plague the scrub woods
beyond Cantrell's pond.

Or a mourning dove, hard to tell. (Question or lament,
question or lament?)

Branches slapped the roof and sides of the tree house.
Light fell
in thin slices through the oak

and dimmed away in the shadows. The woods beyond the pond
dimmed away, then the pond,
then the yard.
                    Spiders took to their corners,
roaches to their corners. Traffic thinned slowly on the highway.

Then the screech owl would startle the scrub woods.

Soon someone else would call, someone from the house.
But I'd not answer. Not yet. I liked to hide.
I liked to sit alone in the dark.

No one knew where to find me. Still,
if I held my breath for a moment, if I stayed quiet, if I listened
and didn't breathe,

a wind might rise and garble my name.

2

You could hardly breathe.

In a corner of the hayloft, where a thin ray of light
from a grimy window fell once a day
in mid-afternoon
and drew across the loft a quivering veil of dust,
you became almost breathless.

Behind a few tattered hay bales
and moldy bags of oats,
you could, in those days, feel a credible silence.
(Careful, though! The feed chutes!)

One Sunday, when I was a boy,
my uncle took me there and draped his jacket
across a sturdy bale.

We used it as a pew, and the prayer he spoke rose
and faded into the rafters.
He lifted a finger to his lips, as if to say *Listen*.

(Silence is the language of faith.) Suddenly, at that sign,

no whistling through windows
of horse stalls, no rasping of floor boards, no worry
of cross-beams propping up rafters and roof.

3

A deep green cave of branches. A leafy darkness.
Something waiting to be born?

I'd sit beside the trunk and gaze up. On clear days patches
of blue ragged
through the upper branches. (Enough to make a sailor's suit?)

In a light rain the green leaves sparkled,
and once I found a glossy snakeskin draped
in a low fork.

But at Christmas the branches sparkled with electric bulbs—
red, green, and blue
and the yellow of traffic lights. My father climbed a ladder
and strung them all the way to the top.

Taller than the house, its leaves were as wide
as a small boy's head, its cones
as large as a football.

I was a small nervous boy.
I liked to hide
and nurture my prayers in dusty places.

Under the skirts
of my grandmother's magnolia, a gentleness sat in.

A gentleness
is all I knew to call it, a calm, a solitude.

Always the Temptation to Abide
~ Daniel Bourne

What is on this street? White car, white car, dirty silver car, red.
But if I want to describe the gilded script

on the blue door to the Ossolineum, the design
like embroided slippers

a Caucasian prince brings to his captured beloved, or the rococo geometry
involved in the sketch of a Renaissance siege machine, tower

that means doom to someone
not remembered in the story?

(*And who in America knows
what Ossolineum means anyway?*)

Meanwhile,
the black tiptap of a young woman's heels

negotiate the small tiles of the sidewalk, the end-of-the-world blast
of an ambulance trying to make it through traffic, angioplasty

for the clogged veins of Herr Burgermeister Wrocław, alarm
and more alarm, crying for us all. Then the slap

of a linden leaf
falling on the sleeve of my overworked arm, trying and trying

to get this one day down. And did I mention that on the way home
I saw a man with his head like a question mark

suspended up against a wall
in front of the Monopolowy Liquor Store—

an ambulance blocking traffic
so that no one was getting home?

(*As it is in memory*
so it is in heaven.)

The cigarette butts
that the city breeds like pigeons.

To Janet in Jersey
~ Julie Bruck

> *Dear Abby: Is it OK to put a paper towel holder in the bathroom?*
> —Janet in Jersey

Don't ever hide your Bounty under the sink. Nor
your conflicted feelings about family members:
Remember the midwife who handed the fawning new parents
their wet, perfect baby? She also told them, "In six months,
when you want to drop this child from a window, call me."
Drink, Janet. Smoke, if it calms you. Take secret joy
in the failings of those who judge you. Judge them back,
if it gives you ballast. When you argue with your dead,
slap anyone who uses the word *closure*. Rail, Janet,
rage about the body's small betrayals: You know
they're only practice for the big one to come. If others
are steeped in denial, that's their problem. Pass gas.
Should someone try to instruct you in The Art of Breathing,
cut that person off for good. Chew your nails. Cheat at cards.
If you would like a roll of paper towels in your bathroom,
Janet in Jersey, you'll get no argument from me. Fuck, yes!

Beneath the Clouds—On Borrowed Time
~ Christopher Buckley

You're living the cliché—
barely a moment
for the thin grace
of altocumulus,
white and liturgical,
or dull as the sand
at high tide....
Not half a chance
to re-read the fine print
that doesn't extend
the warranty, the lifeline ...
actuaries, in their grey
monks' robes having calculated
the return on coverage,
down to each unseen
quark or muon,
our every associated iota
which will be called back
to rattle around
in who knows what
portion of the black
can of creation ...
the universe racing—
by our latest count—
for close to 14 billion years
to pull itself apart
somewhere else....

Like a child walking
through long museum halls,
the faces of your family

pass from sight, gone
with the great masters
into the high self-portraits
hung in the halls of clouds,
held then only in mists
rising through the loose
atmosphere of the mind....

As for the nebulous
swirl of the Aurora Borealis
at the edge of our air,
most of the time
it's barely visible
to the naked eye,
yet now and then bright enough
to read a newspaper by
at night. It's not a dance
of the spirits
as the Cree had it,
nor a sign from God
as medieval Europeans
believed ... the slow
shimmering geomagnetic
waves barely interrupt
the radio, which no one
listens to anymore....
Crosswind, starched-white streets
of cumulus, razor blade
of light at the horizon
and you have your blank map
tossed out again on the blue.

Add some altostratus, thin
inscriptions, un-translatable
as ever....
       Cross the sticks
and stones of childhood
off your list, cross off middle age ...
and even if you can still hear
Ben Webster's *Time On My Hands*,
you only have ghosted exhalations,
the wispy striations
like beamed notes
on the fading sheet music
of the sky. Here you are,
where nothing returns
beyond the insubstantial
gratuities of light,
the capriccios of wind,
nothing beyond whitecaps
whipped up and gone,
marking the lost way out ...
a low marine layer hugging
the coast, lining the road
ahead, a reflection
of our fears undisguised,
and you haven't got a prayer.

The Original Lobster-Eater
~ Cathleen Calbert

The day was long and gray, before ordinary sunshine
and cheerful seabirds. The man's stomach curled inwards.

Yep, he looked like a sick cat. Except there were no cats.
Out of the sea: gelatinous bits of jellyfish and algae.

Nothing much, that is. Then: orange and blue, a puzzle
scuttling towards him, madly, wonderfully, his friend,

his enemy, who knew? This could be his dog, Piggsly.
He'd wrench the seaweed into a leash and teach the creature

tricks. If the man invented slippers, Piggsly could bring them.
Or a sex toy? He rubbed the armored body against his

crotch as he had the coconuts and cacti. A claw; balls:
the usual gotcha moment. In righteous anger, the man

bit off that Hellboy arm and found it good. Chewing up
what could have been a zizzle-bump or Mr. Piggins

seemed perversely pleasurable like drinking squids' ink
or licking the furry second face between his woman's legs.

He never wanted to think about it, so he didn't. Instead,
he invented the word *epicure*, then he awaited the *soufflé*.

Bees
~ Peter Campion

Commissioned for the installation *Meteor Stream* by Terry Adkins
and dedicated to his memory

Wherever the assemblage
re-assembles
        may there be
this video screen
            surrounded by the hanging
maps of Harper's Ferry:
cell on cell
down squiggled streets
accruing round the arsenal.

And may the whole screen be
      a clump of bees.

Because John Brown code-named his raid
"The Hiving of the Bees."
                Because
the bees in their bee-loud glades in poems
straining honey sweet with thyme
stand for the state: collecting
electrostatic drive
to shatter to create.
            Because
when the hero madman hears
his mother in his dream
(her blonde fur molting black)
he sees her
conjure
     sinuous from air

mirages of a fortress grown
to wonder cabinet:
                        casements for
starfish   wolf pelt   saxophone.

Because o queen
                        where networked cells
chain families in their thrall

where madman and hero turned
the same   turned
"meteor of war"

he heard your command:

"bite down the wall."

Gaze
~ Maxine Chernoff

The earliest pilgrims shared a cathedral for a heart.
—Jeanette Winterson

To be the camera for your gaze,
I made myself a candle and a view,
a wish and furtive trees just to the right.
The window, dressed in black, was lifted
like a carpet toward the sky, and feathers
blinked and swarmed around a body meant
to signal flight. The house arrayed for
mourning was too full of ghosts and glass
to feel the ancient history of floorboards'
prelude and retreat. Harsh light filled
the closet with misgivings. Absent
of words, pages were relief from hasty,
moonlit vows. The world, once beaded
with desire, was pale milk-white.
Paper moths were thrown into the fray.

Dragon Jar
~ Patricia Clark

I never wanted to be that fat
with child—don't ask me

how I knew—trusting my gut
in my late twenties due to a dream.

Pale celadon, this, and Korean. I've been
to Seoul, bending to pick up a piece

of crazed greenish pottery in a garden bed
outside the National Museum. We're all

fragments—my dream featured someone
writing in a car window's fog,

letters spelling the word *aim*. See, the jar
stands with swelling sides, an underglaze

of iron brown, from the Yi
Dynasty, and the dragon's coils seem

snakelike. Note how, near the head, it's wearing
either a topknot or a beard. From the dream

on, she crafted a life of her choosing, each day
another dish steaming from the table. Maybe now

I could explain to my mother, she
of the dragon breath, "Oh love, it was never

about you!" And the storage jar held what,
you say? Water, or more luckily, some wine—

and often, of those departed, ashes, purified bone.

My Personal History
~ Andrea Cohen

To guess it is to guess the number
of jelly beans in the basket and if
you guess right (or rightest), to win
the jelly beans, which look like
a rainbow cut up and packaged
for express delivery and guess what—
you don't like jelly beans or rainbows,
or you do, but you suffer
from color-blindness or diabetes and you
know that my personal history gets
boring around page eight, when I start
to explain the scars, which are
layered on top of all the other
scars you've met: some you won
in a contest, some were consolation
prizes. First prize is always the shoulder
to sigh on. Scott Blonder, when I
was six and immortal, dared me to slide
down the water slide into the kidney-
shaped pool. If you do, he said,
Cocoa the poodle will bite you.
I did, Cocoa did, and Mrs. Blonder,
with orange merthiolate, painted a butterfly
on my left thigh. I can't show you
the butterfly, but I can show you its flight
pattern: away. That's how things find
their shape. There's a distance and we
get in line to funnel through it. You
can guess how many of us line up
at once, whether it's more or less
than the number of terracotta warriors

buried with their emperor. I saw
those figures exhibited in Brussels
last year, but they turned out to be
replicas, and who wants to pay
to see a replica of a replica? I've
got mirrors. I've got a personal history
with lint and layaway and oil fed
mistakenly into a basement
with a gas furnace. Things
blow up. Why am I telling you
this? Because dust is trying
to colonize my empire, because
I still have a few sleeves to fill
with tricks. Because I want you
to saw me in half in that French
construction worker's outfit you have
and then put me back together without
letting on that you've never done this
kind of thing before. I want this to be
something we laugh about before
it happens and afterwards, something
to amuse the deep snows long
after our coming and going.

For a Theophoric Figure
~ Peter Cole

Allen Grossman, *in memoriam* (1935–2014)

Strange how first things dawn on us
    late in the game,
                again and again.
Just last week, for instance,
                    I learned
of a young man's lines that appeared on a page,
black flames on a blaze of white—
    early June,
              the year I was born:
The bell pursues me, they said, *it is time …*
    to sigh in the ears of my children.
                    They did,
and do still, though their maker has died,
    and I, a scribe to that living word
he carried toward his distant God
    across diasporas of imperfection,
try now to lift it ever
    so slightly higher, or longer on high,
to honor,
              as I'm able, that force
    he rode for the span of more than his life
out of the Eden of his mind like a river....

Open for Business
~ Peter Cole

1.

Not to see through a scrim—
    though maybe in a simulacrum.
    Not to list or listen
    one's way into something that might have been.
    Not to live in abstract deferment
    but only to sound the lines we're in—
    the music their graphing makes, regardless
    of where that takes us, say,
    into a space where I've been remiss,
    or others dismiss.
        Always to stay open for business.

2.

Always to stay open for business
    in this *isness*, no matter the mess
    one stumbles into. Whatever the mask
    one's face is strung through.
    There *is* a blessing in this being
    not just you. Eventually. It's also true,
    you do want to become who you are,
    or at least be seen as such—
    although it might not take you far.
    Still, this much we can try to do
        for you. Now. Whoever you are ...

3.

For you, now, whoever you are,
    hovering in your penumbral nature,
    shimmering in the pitch of address
    to yourself as someone else:
    Sounds aren't strung along the lines
    of thinking, so much as thought's defined,
    for an instant, by a sense—
    this one sinking   into your voice
    and leaving you nothing in the way of choice
    except to shout out from a crouch that
        you've assumed in the face of assault.

4.

You've assumed in the face of assault
    that in fact it's not your fault.
    Sound did it to you—listening.
    Laboring, well, the minute particulars
    of cadence and pitch and intonation.
    A surface tensility akin to a quality
    or texture combining with taste in the mouth,
    suddenly altering the air in your ear.
    Actually, it's fear speaking
    from within, and that just goes to show you
        that everything out there is also an inkling.

5.

That everything out there is also an inkling
     isn't something I'd been thinking of—
       but here it is inside my morning,
     linking things without my knowing,
     or really trying to. An inkling isn't
     actually within, although it seems so.
Nor does it really involve any ink,
     beyond the letters you're blinking at now.
Often it feels like it's trying to figure
     its way out of a certain darkness.
          At times it even counts as distress.

6.

At times it even counts as distress
     when what's withheld should be about,
       but isn't. Or, when what's ever-so-vaguely beyond—
     is something we've desperately tried to possess.
Mostly that wanting is what defines us,
     and words manage our restlessness.
They're what we do our wanting with, said the
     therapist, strumming our interest in all of this.
In all of this, there's something humming,
     like an engine that needs—not to be fixed,
        only adjusted, for time's nicks, and tricks.

7.

Only adjusted for time's nicks and tricks
    can one really be seen to be someone,
    by which I mean: the Many makes us
    the one we're becoming. And aren't. It takes us through
    whatever we were, and possibly past what
    we might have turned into. And, thank the gods
    of our fathers' mothers, or their brothers'
    family trees—it seems to shake us
    out of its sleeves. So everything feels
    at once both given and chosen. And this, too,
        is one of those tricks that the Many can do.

8.

Is one of those tricks that the Many can do
    something you might try at home
    on your own? Don't be foolish.
    Tricks will happen in any event,
    without your having to do a thing,
    but pay attention, which seems like everything.
    Then again, they rarely occur
    unless your focus is elsewhere—not exactly
    on vacation, but, for instance, facing
    a deep blue dish with a Fasi pattern,
        encoding a faith in fate's sleight-of-hand.

9.

Encoding a faith in fate's sleight-of-hand
    seems like a disciplined sort of insouciance.
    It *has* produced, at any rate, extraordinary
faience. Candy for the eyes of some,
    for others— a metaphysical emblem....
    Like these lines, you might be thinking,
    with them, if everything's coming along
    as I think I'd like it to. Now there's a pause
    in the composition   a waiting for a second
    wind, or inspiration—something to do
        with paradox riding its cause into song.

10.

With paradox riding its cause into song,
    what—ducking, as he said it—he mused,
    could *possibly* go wrong? And when it did,
    he'd chalk it up to the greater gear-work
    of Lady Wisdom's endless lessons,
    in which whatever would be would
    always—maybe—be for the better.
    Such was the mystery of her linking letters.
    But in that possibly—was it true?
    The summer's rubble filled with children.
        Where was Lady Wisdom then?

11.
"Where was Lady Wisdom then"
    is something Job's readers have wondered,
    finding her blurred among his friends,
    abused and elusive in their vapor.
    Though what she knows goes right through them.
    She's like a poem, not some palm
    marking the start of a kind of oasis,
    akin to an answer that one might have missed.
    She weighs amazement with all that is—
    and sees us   back into the welter and gist
        of a being always open for business.

Many Moons
~ Billy Collins

The thinnest of slivers can come
as a surprise some nights.
A girl leaving a restaurant
points up to show her friends.

And there's the full moon,
bloated with light,
a bright circle over the city,
leaving dreamers with no thoughts.

But the moon tonight,
is crossed by a drift of clouds,
and looks like a mug shot
of a bruised man, a grimace for a mouth.

And the frown formed by one of its seas
carries such a wounded look
you would think the last thing
it ever wanted was to be a moon.

It's the sole body in the sky
save for a solitary star,
whose millions of sisters and brothers
must be twinkling somewhere afar,

so I keep one eye on the moon,
the two of us rotating in our turning places,
his face remote and cold,
mine warm but vexed by his troubles.

Shackled
~ Martha Collins

body casts   of ash and pumice

crouching man   man on stairs

Vesuvius trapped   shackled man

Adidas withdrew plans to sell
sneakers with rubber shackles

yellow   slave-shoes

Romans enslaved Greeks
Etruscans   Jews   Anglo-Saxons

—*from Old English* sceacel
(*connection with* shake *unlikely*)

sold   shackled   packed

in ships   thousands   tossed

weighted   with stones   most

unpacked   unloaded   sold

freed slaves to re-enslaved prisoners
shackled together a long chain

to civil rights to back in your place
to shackles back in fashion

for $49.99 on eBay:
antique shackles rare forged iron women's slave

also *naut*: pin may be captive, married to shackle

also sexual: shackles sold online

wanted   want

The Flight into Egypt
~ Peter Cooley

In the tradition of the Old Masters,
who painted the threesome and the obliging mule,
in their Italian hills, I have placed mine
luminous in our New Orleans winter.

How safe my city keeps them. No one
questions their passing through the French Quarter:
infant, teenage mother, bald Joseph her father's age.
They're just more rag-tag wayfarers down here.

And you who watch them, staring out at you,
now that I've turned their heads, even the mule's—
does your millennium allow you one radiant-still moment?
Do you, ten thousand fourteen, still believe?

When the Conductor Disappeared
~ Tom Crawford

It's such a relief to be going nowhere.
Knowledge weighed like a suitcase.
So long to get here. A long train,
I'm telling you it was long. For years
people got on and people got off.
Then, gradually the wheels slowed.
Last station or maybe the one before,
the conductor punching tickets
just disappeared, I mean altogether.
Oh, how that lightened the load,
the noise of those terrible knuckles
banging, the screeching wheels.
The last jolt must have awakened me.
Now, all the cars, empty to play in …
nothing to be, and it just gets better,
for lunch I had a mayonnaise and baloney
sandwich on bad white bread.
Oh my, just to think all that time
I thought I was awake
going somewhere.
It was like sleeping every night—
such a waste of stars.

White Room
~ Cynthia Cruz

In the sanitarium, starving
Simone Weil.

What a beautiful room, she said,
To die in.

Delirious, on her deathbed,
Listing off

The miraculous
Banquet of her childhood.

French bread, and butter
Soup, mashed potatoes,

Roast lamb in mint,
Thick cream,

And fruit tarts made by her mother,
With milk.

Her last word on this earth
Was *Nurses*.

But, where
Does God live?

Inside the blind wound
Of our hearts.

Pressing Help
~ Jim Daniels

My parents sleep in separate rooms
at 87. Last week my blind mother lay
in so much pain she could not rise
to rouse my half-death father.
I mean half-deaf.

She thought at first she might
just let herself die, but it hurt
too much. She pressed the HELP button
I'd insisted she wear. She called it
her collar.

They're not good at ceding
control, though I might not be any better
toeing that wobbly line. She often
forgets it. The BUTTON. We capitalize
half our conversations

these days to accommodate facilitate
motivate or simply to be heard.
Come here, Mother, yes, that's
a good girl. Sit. Stay. Don't try to roll over.
The BUTTON calls HELP and HELP

calls back. My father answers,
gets up to check, finds my mother
in so much pain she used the button!
I don't know where the HELP

people work. The hospital kept her.
She said the stay was a nice distraction

from her daily life. Maybe she said
vacation. Definition shrinks,
then evaporates.

Maybe she'll get so bored, she'll press
The BUTTON again. We, her children
are counting on it. My father? Is he
listening, his ear to what's become
of her golden necklace? He admires
her heart.

Old Blood Rising
~ Jim Daniels

Remember when you flicked your wrist
in my direction—slanting snow sifting down
magic through streetlight glow? Some questions
we hope go unanswered, but we ask them
anyway. Magic? Really?—

walking on the other side
of West Center with that guy
you dumped me for that you've been
married to for thirty years now. I admit
I was kneeling in the snow begging you
to come back, my nose hairs frozen
in sub-zero self-pity. If I saw you again
I'd tell you that was my idea of a joke.

Because how could we ever go back
down there, the dark vault of betrayal,
my faux suicide, tears and snot,
kids blowing up things, thinking
that's what love did.

Remember those great orgasms
we had in the basement
on my father's warped pool table,
bringing each other off, hands
shoved down each other's tight jeans?
Those rafters never looked so good
as we swallowed sighs and listened
for each upstairs creak.

He was a creep back then, but I'm sure
he's matured in thirty years and lost
his hair. See, I'm full of jokes.

Today walking in Shaw Park
where we used to—you know—
I ran into my own kid in flecto dilecto
under the bridge with a young partner,

and I remembered. Our lives sucked,
we always used to say. We're old
enough to have ghosts and tender moments.

Remember? When's the last time you saw
an ink eraser? All they did was tear the paper
to shreds When's the last time you saw a hickie?

Maybe that's what we needed to do,
rip up the damn paper and be done
with it. But they didn't teach us how
in gym class or Michigan History
or Outdoor Chef or Homemaking.

Marking each other's necks with blood
and pledging eternal everything, burning
ourselves with the magnifying glass
and blaming the sun, in lieu of.

I would tell you that I kept walking
over that low bridge above my man-child
beneath me, thinking they must be cold
down there, hoping they were sighing

not crying. We take our magic
where we can get it, and it's often
(always?) dark magic. *I should have.*

I hate when I start saying that.
Nothing good comes of it. Boy
in the snow, get off your knees,
damn it. Save those knees.
Plenty more things to beg for
down the line.

My hands were cold
on that bridge. I reminded
myself that memory can't be
one long apology. I tilted
my neck toward the sky,
offering it up.

Debt
~ Kwame Dawes

What is owed us, our bodies slumping
from years of labor, the promise of longevity
a lie? We cannot count the years
like others, so we flame in those
early years when our bodies are reliable,
when our strength can let us be
beaten, used and we bounce back,
belies full of laugh, fists swinging,
this is all it is. At forty, we are
limping, the calculation is basic,
ten more years if we are lucky.
These are the times to make amends
for the wounds we learn to cry,
learn to say, "Don't leave me," learn
to drink in the dark, feel the rumbling
of death, learn to stare
at a wall for hours, to know
how comforting this emptying
of the brain can be, this silence,
how memory, played out in such
silences, can soothe. What is owed
this man with big arms, useless
shoulders, and dick that has
forgotten its own nature, a man
who has lived on the edge
of grand things? What is owed
him but his daily wage for
his labors, a safe path to walk
each day, the right to gather as a man
among men, get drunk, skip it off
and stare at walls, counting the days?

She is dead, the girl who carried
his seed; he has broken her. How happy
he was to see her glow with the swell
of the child in her, and then the way
she slipped away, a mattress soaked
in blood, the baby girl wailing,
his hands too clumsy to hold this
flesh; what is owed an ordinary
black man with nothing to show
for his life? In the dark, the wounded
wife planting geraniums and singing
hymns in the dark loamed garden,
the infant girl giggling in the sunlight,
the earth turning slowly; he allows
the blanket to cover him, travels
to the open lot of a ballpark, dust
dancing in the air, a clean sky
and the scent of mown grass—
this is all he is owed today.

Hunters
~ Carl Dennis

If my father had been a hunter
And had taught me to think of gun lore
As a part of wood lore, I might not regard
All hunters as killers, even if hunting had proved
For me, after a season a two,
A joyless pastime: transforming a deer
Bounding across a clearing or pausing
To catch a sound or a scent into a carcass.

I might have abandoned the practice
Without any rancor, as I might have abandoned
My imagined father's distrust of government
Or his faith in a creed that offered salvation
Only to those baptized according to rules
Revealed to just one church, his own.

I might have done justice to his belief
He was doing the deer a service
By thinning the herd so it wasn't so large
It starved when the snow lay deep.
I might have praised his effort to protect
Half the herd's habitat from a mall expansion.

I'd want to distinguish a thoughtful hunter like him
From those who delight in driving through town
With a dead deer draped on the hood
As if they were braves flashing a string of scalps
As proof of their manly defense of the tribe
Against marauding parties of enemies.

It takes a brave man, and a knowing one,
To leave behind the weapon that makes him
An angel of death to the herds, if not a god,
And follow them undetected on their retreat
Into the underbrush, like a reporter sent
To report on a local, reclusive tribe
Not available for a photo shoot or an interview.

Big news from the woods in the first installment
Of a ten-part series that not one deer
Appears unhappy to be a deer.
Not one would prefer to be a bear or a cougar.
Not one is sorry it's not a man.

Selected Poems by W. S. Di Piero

Photograph by Beth Weber

Interview with W. S. Di Piero
conducted by *Plume* Associate Editor
for Special Projects, Nancy Mitchell

NM: In preparation for this Featured Selection, I read several of your prose pieces, including "San Francisco" and "Semba!: A Notebook," both from the Poetry Foundation website. I was struck by the particularly musical, surging, ambulatory rhythm of "San Francisco"; I had the sensation of sprinting to catch a rickshaw, or a similar means of jaunty, open air conveyance, which once caught, carried me along at a nice clip through enchantingly bizarre landscapes, all the while narrated by a roguishly witty tour guide. It reminded me of a friend's description of the Burning Man festival.

In comparison, the tempo in "Semba!" is slower; not quite adagio … your perspective, circumscribed by heavy rain, comes from a physical interior, and from the interior of the self; each equally palpable. The sections seem to be spoken from various depths of this interior, so the piece as a whole is almost like a fugue. There is so much poetry in your prose, I felt both centered and off balance; a lovely sensation, which I was thrilled to experience again when I turned to these poems. I'm curious, how much do you draw from your notebooks for poems?

W. S. Di P: A lot of material in "San Francisco" and "Semba!" came straight out of my notebooks; some was worked up for the occasion. I'd been asked by *Poetry* magazine to write about city walking, so I went at it, but my local life ordinarily gets into the notebooks, too, so I lifted some documentary stuff there. For "Semba!," I mentioned to *Poetry*'s then-editor, Christian Wiman, that I was trying to empanel bits and chunks from my notebooks into something that would (maybe) have its own coherence, and he asked to see it. At that point, once I knew the entries would be worked up to form a network, I became more methodical in the choosing and sequencing, more than I ever am when I'm just filling up the notebooks. I started to mess a little with what I had, to refine, build up, reduce. The separate parts of *Poems from Notebooks* either started in the notebooks or at some point got transcribed there. I'd written the parts over a period of a few years, at least, so it's hard to reconstruct their individual histories. What mattered to me was the insistence, within and among the parts, of the dispatches of consciousness. Everything—poems, notebooks, poems begun in notebooks, notebook-like poems that never appear in notebooks—everything speaks to everything else.

NM: You are amazingly and intimidatingly prolific, especially for a writer like myself, for whom almost every word is a pathetic, little agony—your writing seems to move with such enviable ease, fluidity between genres, and with inclusive generosity, intimacy. How do you achieve this somewhat fearless grace?

W. S. Di P: Prolific? I wish. I've always wanted greater fluency, greater ease. I'm never satisfied with anything, certainly not with the *amount* of work I've done. A prose poem in *Nitro Nights*, "To Fear," is my invocation to fear. The grace you mention is more likely a consequence, not a companion, of the fear. As for "inclusive intimacy," yes, I've aspired to that, but it all has to happen in the action of the words. Moral or emotional sincerity is admirable but doesn't usually make for good art. (Moral or emotional rawness, ambiguity, ardor—well, that's different.) The "fluidity between genres" is probably due to my lifetime's practice: I've written prose of one sort or another (except fiction) for as long as I've written poetry. There's some mysterious organic difference between prose—whether it's autobiography, journalism, criticism—and poetry. It has to do with the formal dynamics, the temperatures of intensity: poetry has in its magnitudes expressive powers beyond those of prose, though the number of those powers, the count, may be fewer.

NM: Yes; maybe the formal dynamics create the electricity … all that molecular energy vibrating between words, sounds, and line breaks, in the white space between stanzas. Yet there is that electricity in your prose and between your prose and poetry, a kind of concentric circuitry, if you will, not unlike that of "The musician from Mali/ plucks his kora…" from "On the Radio" in the selection below.

Your writing seems to be a self-contained, self-sustaining ecology; as you write earlier, "Everything—poems, notebooks, poems begun in notebooks, notebook-like poems that never appear in notebooks— everything, in my practice, speaks to everything else." Robust and remarkably generative… although I suppose generative isn't the right word…structurally it isn't a family tree… but rather a Fibonacci spiral. Can you speak to this?

W. S. Di P: It's gratifying to hear that. I believe the human imagination possesses radical forms and behaviors, which is why the old stories in Ovid and Homer are so tenacious and awful. The imaginations of individual poets articulate local, idiosyncratic expressions of those forms and behaviors. Those are, I think, what you're calling ecologies: any one piece of the system will have something to say to some other piece and exist in a particular relation to it. *Poems from Notebooks* took many shapes as I kept writing at it. The pieces started out as separate poems, then I realized that I was writing, really, in some of the poems, about squirmy, convulsive sexuality. I wrote the Miró poem to cry out sexual force fields. It's an homage to him and all the aroused stuff in his pictures.

NM: I was wondering if this conversation, in which "one piece of the system will have something to say to some other piece and exist in a particular relation to it," and "the insistence, within and among the parts, of the dispatches of consciousness" is the webby glue, if you will, the coherence between all your writing?

W. S.Di P: My work has a kind of liquid or runny coherence. I'm an associative poet, I'm not very deliberative, I don't feel I have to explain anything. My task is to register and interrogate the patterns of meaning I feel around me every day. In "The Settlements," for instance, I wanted to get down—to recognize, not analyze—a sudden, happenstance moment when that field of relatedness asserts itself. It happens, it's history, just like that. "Mackerel in the Sea" for me is a delirium of resemblances. These things happen to me: the poems are my answering to their interventions in my life.

NM: Lovely; thank you. Let's us now turn to these interrogations, these answerings.

from *Poems from Notebooks*
~ W. S. Di Piero

IN THE KITCHEN

We talk about how
    our words seem
to come between us.
    The paring knife slips,
slices a thumbnail,
    garlic half-moons fall,
blood arcs on the bamboo,
    lightning lights up
the dark broken sky
    and shocks the asphalt shingles,
we chase the lightning down
    by talking faster.

HE SAYS SHE SAYS

Love, sex love I mean, is predatory.
        That's what we're born and meant for.
                It's never nice. Desire eats us up
                        and we eat it up and never finish.

                        Kittiwake, kingfisher, kite,
                a magpie's blacks and whites
        on blacktop in the redwoods.
Do you see what I see?

MACKEREL IN THE SEA

are in the sky where they look like
  the sandy ribs the tide has left behind,
and farther out on the sea's oiled surface lies
  a mackerel skin the sun loves to lick.
Here along my streets are mackerel scales
  of rain and lights that stripe the air:
the fog detests their sharper edges,
  the winter cold eats them up.
Our candlelight inside the rain that's running
  down the window, where we find ourselves,
   holds mackerel that are schooling out at sea.

THE SETTLEMENTS

My cab driver can't shut up
about all this silly self stuff,
who needs it when you believe?
You pray, the voice of God
will be there for us but
life is life anyway, yes?
He left wife and kids behind
in Palestine, ten years now,
money for them, I need the money,
a kidney transplant, shoes, teeth,
pray for me, my friend,
because He meant for you
to be here, to pray for me.

On the Radio

The musician from Mali
plucks his kora, picks at
our nerves, the strings
run through navel to groin
to heel and toe as if
the body could lift itself
out of body even while
the sound wires itself
deeper than we've gone
inside our own selves:
its hairy roots push down,
grip tighter inside us,
reaching for darker water
running underground.

TO JOAN MIRÓ, DB, BILLIE MIRÓ, THELONIUS BLUE,
AND A FEW FRIENDS

Fins and feathers.
Bowels and blood.
Our night sky blued,
its star-buds and lures
and black banana boat
and constellation of fish
fornicating a cloud,
its kite of a red moon-
scythe now the face
that is a sandy hill.
Pubes and pups.
Teardrops and tracks.

THE TIME OF DAY

They are inspiration without purpose,
the cut shades of ravens in the sun,
under the sun, in morning's tender light.

They sail and shrink across tarred roofs,
their black now blacker sailing there,
the flight of shadows that cannot fly,

an astonishment on the wing of the air,
shades of no underworld that go in search
of shadows they do not know the shapes of yet.

IN THE PAST

We live into the pauses, love,
and the places we've left behind
coat our bodies as if with
cobwebbed air or foam that
we feel faithful and tickly,
somehow even taste
on each other's flesh
but can't clearly see.

AND JUST LIKE THAT

like sea swimmers
        shaking their violent hair,
the city cypresses
        from the cold tips
of their tough needles
        shake loose in the wind
black brittle drops
        that prickle the night air,
lit inside by ardent
        bearded streetlamps.

THE MOTION

The ravens roust the red-tail,
its redness fills and flails the window,
the sun barks their smart blackness

and cut-outs houses, backyards—
the sun that moves around us
while we move around its fires.

The Swallows
~ W. S. Di Piero

For you, naturally, only for you
and your love of growing things
plain and sumptuous, and now,
from that hysterical earnest florist
on Via Ugo Bassi, near Burger King,
rowdy debonair ranunculi for you,
and Signor Histerica Passio declared,
Ranuncoli olandesi! Importantissimo,
somehow, the Holland angle
we teased out through dinner,
those bloody blackred fisty blooms
I carried in my fist, as instructed,
upside down, to drain their biojuices
into stems, pistils, bloom-tissue,
as if to bait a grasping underworld,
to enliven and keep them fresh
the two smart blocks to your address,
where we set them on the terrace,
earthy-heavy between us and our
forty-year friendship. "We live
more than one life, we live a few,
they come and go, one and one,
we come and go, this life to that."
The city's inflamed roof tiles cooled
below us in the twilight sky:
the sulfur streetlamps pinked
Via dell'Inferno's cobblestones.

The watchful flowers darkened, too,
as we darkened, beside the rosemary
and gardenias, the moist stink of turned soil
insidious among the aroused sweet scents,
while above us (remember?) around
the two ancient towers, the swallows
chased and fled their own whistling.

for Cicci

"What a Fabulous View You Have"
~ W. S. Di Piero

Some houses start to tick alive with lamps.
The hospital's white windows don't flinch.
Parnassus Ave., down below, arches its back:
your finger, in those years, traced its spine
up and down my unwashed windows. The sea
gives off pinky particulate vapors. No sun yet.
The moon's full, Shiva's moon of ways and ends.

You changed the ways. My new habit's yours.
Your mousey hours, pushing 3 a.m.
when you went to bed, were three hours short
of when I used to wake to start my day,
start the work. That old me left home with you.
Your rhythms outlived us: now I'm up late
like you, sleep two hours, then am up again,

like now, before I hit my second sleep:
the radio tower's pulsing red lights plead
unconsoling constancy: one house,
invisible in the woods below, ignites
a cat's-cradle of crystal lights that pop
in zany sequences, like happiness
or alarm or something worse. It's October,

I look to find someone like me looking out
and back at me from windows across the way.
The fake snow of rooftops painted white glows

in dull remnant moonlight that also fell
on those air plants you brought to me and to
this garden of a kitchen of work, its fruit, knives, CDs,
unruly pages, dear screen, old address books …

In time, the garden-center lady said, they'll bloom,
but give them tons of direct sunlight.
They bloomed but didn't last. Their fuzzy skin
made you want to pet them. I'm marking time,
saying nothing, really, except I feel
I've assumed your watch, this hour of this world,
and will pay attention to whatever stirs.

Which Aisle?
~ W. S. Di Piero

I'm making Lady Hardware sad.
She's noble in her fuschia smock
and grayed, pinned-up hair, and loves
the title I've conferred on her.
She's bummed because today I've brought,
broken from a neighbor's tree,
sprigs of the life of western things,
the labials of mock-oranges,
such dirty trees, but I don't care,
because they're the end of the world.
I offer them to her large nose,
she shuts her eyes, she's in Eden.
No. No. "Yes I can," I say and sing
"*I certainly can can-can,*"
anything to lighten our mood,
because she can tell how lost I am
to my errand's hopelessness.
"I want this, I have to have this
in my apartment." No way, big boy.

When I came here in the seventies,
its scent hid inside fog, car lights,
wet winds, fire sirens, pork buns,
I carried it in my nose, on my skin,
I smelled it whenever I chose, I want
all that impacted time and place
with me as these small days run down,

let me keep it, preserve it somehow,
freeze or cork or atomize
the citrusy humid ga-ga drift
that calls back insane florid sex
and hurts my forehead when I inhale.
In an apartment, not a chance,
I'm sorry, honey, but give it up.
She doesn't say: You fool, you,
who doesn't carry lost things?
You're a strange child for a man your age,
but an old man is bound to be a little
off and gone. It's what comes naturally.

Nimrod & The Flying Pig
~ Norman Dubie

1.

The king was burning the tall grasses
to market an exhaust, a gate
animals would spring from, Nimrod's
archers dropping them in air,
in service to the autumn banquet.

It felt nearly a winter's day and the king
looked into the black smoke of the sky
while a green flying sow
passed wildly overhead detailing
to the king that he was shameless
and truly cursed among men.

2.

This pig threw this king off his need
for a harvest mead. He returned
a large cart full of grapes and wheat
to his old toothless mother

3.

who he had imprisoned months earlier
somewhere in the southern swamp.

4.

Nimrod began to fast. He shaved
his head and snorted myrrh with prayers.
Then the pig flew over again, over
Nimrod's bath house
which was open to sky.

The pig told the king once more
that essentially
he was doomed beyond remedy,

more than anyone who'd lived in recorded history.
(This limitation, its specificity
with reference to time emboldened

Nimrod who reached instantly for his bow, piercing
mortally the pig's throat
with a long yellow arrow of pine wood.)

5.

From that day forward the king
lived in perfect happiness
far into old age
and was blessed with six sons
who like their father were also cruel
beyond definition.

The king said *he was individually
charmed among men*. Reports,
in fact, insist that his mother is still
living in a suburb of Annapolis—

'flying pig' is NSA
code for something you'd *seriously*
rather not know. Now,

read our poem to its conclusion
but never tell a single living soul
of your exposure to it.

Oh, and
the pig's name was Protobus.

Protobus is an anagram
of Hamlet. Thelma is an anagram
of Hamlet. Pity the poor pig.
Poor all of us.

The Story of Waves
~ Denise Duhamel

My friend and I stand in the sea, our calves
in cold waves—first wave, second,
third, and now fourth wave feminism.
She is trying to decide
if she should have an affair
to even the score. I am trying to help her

by listing the pros and cons. She despairs
as her husband ogles topless sunbathers.
She herself was once a topless sunbather. But today
my friend and I are clothed, rolled-up jeans,
our body temperatures lowering
in the cold sea. We are middle age, trying

to be logical, dispassionate.
The man with whom she wants to sleep
makes my friend feel like a coquette.
She is sure her husband's lover
was younger and thinner.
Into forever pretty girls

walk by her husband
who turns to watch. My friend and I
are deep in conversation
where anything seems possible—
her divorce, a new life, trysts galore.
Yet she holds back—what if

this new paramour eventually makes her feel
as crappy as her husband
does now? Pessoa wrote,

"An inmate in an insane asylum is at least someone.
I'm an inmate in an asylum without an asylum."
We see the beautiful men on the sand,

their tanned abs and arms, their shorts
and volleyball. My friend does not for a minute
think she could possess them. She admires them

more than desires them. She fastens
her own straight jacket/life vest with humility
and regret until she is invisible,

even to me. She wants to be desired
the way her husband desires
the topless bathers, the way
he thinks he has a right
to possess each young women
in his imagination. The waves bash

our ankles. I am trying to be present,
but feel Antero do Quental's
"infinite air of loneliness,"
the despair that I will never be able
to say what I truly think, even to my friend,
for fear it will make her feel worse.

The other husbands sit in beach chairs
near her husband. They are talking
politics and sports, whistling
at women for fun, while my friend
and I make her every decision
heavy, the way our wet jean cuffs

are now heavy. My guess
is her husband has forgotten
all about her as we obsess
over his blatant indiscretions.
I try to change the subject—movies,
books, the economy, war.

But she keeps coming back
to her fury spiraling like a waterspout.
This is the story of waves.
We once washed ashore, girls full of hope
and lust. Now we have come back afraid,
holding each other's forearms for balance—

frosty queens with icicle earrings,
snow streaking our hair.

Songs Of Hierarchy And Hoodie
~ Denise Duhamel and Maureen Seaton

Z. zeroes in on me in my nightmare, my ZZZ's
yanked away by my own yelps. But youngsters
x-men their way out of xylophonic wars, don't they?
What? White? Who wants to know? Your best friend
vimeo-ed the vagaries of vagabonds vandalizing
umpteen Über cars driven by university undergrads
tripping on Toll House. Tsk. Now a testy task master
steals shindigs and slaloms down Sacajawea's
Road, racing by rodeos, roundups, and ranch hands
quoting Raymond Queneau—"this queer fish was quite bats."
Perhaps Popeye or perhaps Philadelphia. Perhaps
oscillate or on occasion ossify. Olive Oyl too, only
new to Noam Chomsky, never nonchalant.

Memorials accommodate each 9-mm's mistake,
like our land's a land of laws, not justice, woops, don't
kid about the letter J, we're not there yet, kiddo—
just between us, justice is a joke in the 24 Jacksons
in the US, in Ferguson, in Inglewood. Injustice is
howl not hoot, hobble not help, Holy Hitman,
G., grab gossamer, rabid guns are for ghosts
freaking out about their finality, floating for-
ever on the edges of the equinox of epiphany.
Dear Doris Day and Dali Lama, please do not deliver
carloads of que seras to the kids on the corner.
Bodyguard them from bullies and bullets, be
airtight angels adept at ascendance and assistance.

Floridada: Our 51ˢᵗ State
~ Denise Duhamel and Maureen Seaton

Whereas, the new proposed state of South
Florida may float off into the Caribbean
if we wait for Rick Scott, we propose
a divorce. Tallahassee never loved
Okeechobee anyway, and the scary
hurricane thing, well, who needs that?
Whereas, the Turkey Point nuclear reactors
are well past their prime, we insist
on palimony, as we've shipped a lot of loot
north and it's never come back—and our ship
was very dear to us. Tallahassee knows
that! We promised ourselves we wouldn't cry
for 150 years (our ultimate submersion),
but the mangroves are threatening to walk
and the pigeon plums are packing their trunks.
Whereas, the Everglades are on fire
and ghost orchids are hitching rides and
thousands of tree islands stand on tippy toes,
we draw the line at Brevard, Orange, Polk,
Hillsborough and Pinellas. Above that,
there are pelicans to relocate and several feet
of seawater to bail before century's end.
Whereas, our buckets are the plastic kind
we give to our kiddies, we request
a split (not spit), a schism (not prison), and a
big old raft of miracles to save our soggy asses.

Çağrı Merkezi
~ Efe Duyan

hoş geldiniz
okul arkadaşlarınızla tanıştığınız güne dönmek için
lütfen uğurlu sayınızı tuşlayınız
bahçede yorulmaksınız koşturduğunuz zamanlar için
rastgele tüm rakamlara basınız
kamyoncu lokantalarının buharlı camekânları için
ailecek çıkılmış son yaz tatilinin yılını kodlayınız

herkesin vardır çok utandığı anlar
tuttuğunuz rakamı kimseye söylemeyiniz
üniversite çimlerinde çay ve poğaçalı kahvaltılar için
hemen ahizeyi bırakıp balkona çıkınız
zamanın apar topar geçmesinden şikâyetçiyseniz
lütfen tüm gücünüzle sıfıra bastırınız
dedenizi tam hatırlamadığınızı fark ettiyseniz
aynaya bakın lütfen

sahafların tozlu kitap kokusu için
okuma yazma bilmeyen bir işçinin
adındaki üçüncü harfi söyleyiniz
yırtık pırtık elbiseleriyle ölü bulunmuş mahalle terziniz için
lütfen bekleyiniz

uykunuzdaki kadının
boynuna dokunduğunuz o sonrası bilinmez an için
biip sesinden sonra
arka arkaya aynı sayıya basınız

terk edildiğinizin ertesi günü
deftere yüz kere bir daha âşık olmayacağım yazınız

biiip

from *One Poem Stands*
Call Centre
~ Efe Duyan, translated by W. N. Herbert

hello
for the day you met school friends for the first time
please dial your lucky number
for the times you ran tirelessly around the playground
press all the numbers at random
for the steamed-up windows of greasy spoons
dial the year of the last family summer holiday

everybody has times they're ashamed of
do not tell the numbers you pick for these to anyone
for the tea and poğaça breakfasts you had on the university lawn
put the receiver down and go out onto the balcony
if you wish to complain about time flying furiously past
please press down hard on the button
if you realise that you don't remember your granddad exactly as he was
look in the mirror

for the smell of dusty books in second-hand bookstores
say the third letter of an illiterate labourer's name
for your neighbourhood tailor who was found dead in rags
please hold

for that unpredictable moment
that you touched the neck of a woman in your sleep,
dial the same number over and over again
after the beep

the day after the break-up
write in your notebook one hundred times
'I am never going to fall in love again'

beeep

Anonimowi Bohaterowie Dni Ostatnich
~ Tadeusz Dziewanowski

Anonimowi Bohaterowie dni ostatnich

NN 1899–1985, mężczyzna, przeżył 31390 dni ostatnich
Zabił człowieka bagnetem

NN 1666–1709, mężczyzna, przeżył 15706 dni ostatnich
Wiele razy upił się piwem jopenbier,
Zmarł na zarazę

NN 1929–2004, kobieta, przeżyła 27399 dni ostatnich
Spaliła stanik

NN 1944–1964, mężczyzna, przeżył 7305 dni ostatnich
Zjadł trzy hamburgery nad wodospadem Niagara

NN 563–483 pne, mężczyzna, przeżył 29200 dni ostatnich
Siedział pod drzewem uśmiechnięty
Zatruł się pokarmem

NN 1953–?, mężczyzna, dotąd przeżył 19731 dni ostatnich
(Niedawno odkryto, że posługuje się inicjałami TD)
Miał czarnego psa.

Unknown Heroes
~ Tadeusz Dziewanowski, translated by Daniel Bourne

To the Unknown Heroes of the Final Days

NN 1899–1985, male, survived 31,390 final days on earth.
Killed a man with a bayonet.

NN 1666–1709, male, survived 15,706 final days on earth.
Many times he became drunk on Dutch Jopenbier.
Died of the plague.

NN 1929–2004, female, survived 27,399 final days on earth.
Once burned her bra.

NN 1944–1964, male, survived 7,305 final days on earth.
Ate three hamburgers in the vicinity of Niagara Falls.

NN 563–483 B.C.E., male, survived 29,200 final days on earth.
Sat smiling beneath a tree.
Died because of food poisoning.

NN 1953–?, male, survived so far 1,931 final days on earth.
(A recent discovery is his use of the initials TD).
Once owned a black dog.

From Heaven, My Father Sends His Regrets
~ Cornelius Eady

Son, you still don't know squat about fishing.
I couldn't teach you the bait, the hook, how
The line sings, the fuzzy ride to meet the morning.
Explain to me how a boy could turn
Fun away so fast; you so certain you knew stupid
When stupid pulled up at 4 a.m. and your Uncle
And me, we became black sparrows, flashlights burning
Our lawn for worms. All you had to throw back at me
Was stubborn, and stubborn worked. It's what
You forgot when your poems resurrected me
And I turned, in the way you say things, into an oaf. I offered
You a place to wade with me. What do you want,
Now that you're grown, now that you're curious?

Ars Poetica
~ Lynn Emanuel

Poetry doesn't do story—*Who is killing whom and why?* It does bright oblongs of view laminated into perfect stillness: some pale face locked up in the locket of a stanza until it looks enormous. That's what poetry's all about—the immensity of the miniature, the clenched box of the quatrain, lines taped shut by end-rhyme.

It is the bric-a-brac of sound effect. It is emptiness, bandages without wounds, not the evidence, but the locked room you can't get into. Poetry withholds. That's its beauty: nullity and rest. Blue window, blue window, like an island you could swim to—

It could be an escape. And perhaps the only one: the smallest unit into which survival fits. Take its bantam grandeurs anywhere. Even to prison. And if it's dark and cold and no one comes, except the faceless guards and their clubs, even there poetry can erect its subversive insubstantiality. Some scrap of poetry will come into your head, raising its fists. It may be it is the last thing you remember.... *Still the dead one lay moaning/And not waving but drowning.*

The Algorithm Introduced Us
~ Elaine Equi

Now we are inseparable,

virtually indistinguishable
from one another.

Liking the same music,
always ordering our pasta
without cheese.

Buying the same sweaters—
only mine is blue
and yours is red.

Maybe I should get a red one too
and you should get the blue—
just to have, just in case
we change our minds.

Wandering The Wormhole
~ Elaine Equi

Camera in hand—

taking pictures
I've already seen

in books
I've already read.

The stockyards.

Two women
walking casually
arm in arm,

wearing long dresses
with ribbons
and straw hats.

Shadow Puppetry
~ Kathleen Flenniken

Someone's hand grew tired
cutting delicate lacework,

discriminating hemlock
from Douglas fir.

The stage at 3:00 am
is illuminated by spotlight.

Please tell me the play
is about to begin.

If only a bird appeared
from the wings, fluttering

like origami on a wand,
or an empress

who loves a gardener
who will not love her back.

Three coy trees touch bows
like maidens holding hands—

that's all there is of drama.
Not even a car backfires.

I'm tired of the suspense.
Puppeteer, stop hiding

behind your silhouettes.
Reach into my chest.

I'm ready to applaud the wolves.

Heaven Or Hell: Your Choice!
~ Stuart Friebert

the sign along 511 to Kipton says,
where I bike to lunch in the gazebo
near the old granary, its windows
mostly broken so birds fly in & out.
The old depot's gone now, but you
may know about "The Great Kipton
Train Wreck" of 1891; the expression
"on the ball" too, for which we can
thank Webb Ball, the plaque reads,
a jeweler investigating time & watch
conditions throughout the Lake Shore
& Michigan Southern Railway's lines,
who designed a time-keeping program
& watches trainmen still use, after he
concluded one engineer's watch was
"possibly four minutes slow!" #14, a fast
mail train, had collided with the Toledo
Express. (Hell came way too fast for nine
souls who died, but let's hope Heaven
is where they flew to.) Google curator &
historian Nancy Pope for the grisly details.
Then come sit here to watch the birds cut
collages out of the sweet summer air, kids
swinging on the little playground adjacent,
voices pitched to shrieks at times enshrouding
any groans & moans left over from that April
day cars were "telescoped and smashed
to kindling wood, and one rolled over on
the station platform, breaking the depot's
windows." Suddenly my mouth parches,
I can't finish my sandwich, break it to bits

to toss to the birds, one of which ventures
close enough to pet, chirping agreeably.
God was with you, too, I whistle, as if it had
escaped from the cage a little girl held on
her lap in the parlor car before colliding with
#14; a little girl of auburn hair, tiny teardrops
in her eyes, unexpectedly hurtled toward
an awful exclamation, her mother shot off
in another direction, no time to choose be-
tween Heaven or Hell. Well, what's done is
done, but suddenly amid the dead silence
now, you might find it hard to stoop down
at the little spigot the playground kids can't
turn back on quickly enough to slake each
other's thirst, when from somewhere a little
bird, screeching, petrifies in the stony sky.

White Feather
~ Jeff Friedman

After Alexsandra kissed me, a white feather flew out of my mouth. I pretended that nothing out of the ordinary had happened, though the feather floated between us for a long while before it fell on the carpet. The feather was long and bowed with soft fringe. I wanted to pick it up and twirl it, but Alexsandra seemed concerned. "Did you eat a white bird?" she asked. I shook my head. "It's only one feather," I answered. She eyed me suspiciously, though a moment before she had seemed perfectly happy to be kissing me. To prove that there was no problem, I kissed her, and everything was fine. Our lips met, our tongues touched and tangled as they had a thousand times before. Then another feather floated from my mouth and stuck in her thick black hair. She pulled it out and scrutinized the feather for a long time. "There's something inside you trying to get out," she said. "You have to do something about it." "What can I do?" I said. "It's only two feathers." She picked up her journal and began writing. Now I was alarmed. Had I done something to deserve this? Had a bird flown into my mouth in a dream? I thought about my dreams, but couldn't remember anything particular. "Let's try one more kiss," I said, but this time, a white dove flung itself from my mouth, flying wildly around the room until it hit the window and fell on the floor. "Is it dead?" I asked. She kneeled down and cradled the dove in her arms. Then she carried it outside—I thought to bury it, but instead she threw it in air. The dove caught itself before plummeting into the pavement and landed on a branch above us. "We'll figure this out," she said, squeezing my hand, but I could already feel a tickling in my throat as the dove began singing.

Perpetual City
~ Carol Frost

Mixtures of blue and yellow on winter white
walls,

pussy willow arranged in a dry vase,
The Book of Beasts,
sundial, desk waterfall, heron
of teak, bill and chest
shaped of one substance: Thus someone
recreates life after life
inside the city. Yah. Yah. Yah.
On the paved streets weight thrown
on the ball of the foot, while the other thigh
is lifted. To think how walking
confounded mechanical engineers,
their extraordinary patience with the clumsy
first robots. Twelve month and twelve month
after

with cities put to sleep, icebergs melted to nothing,
they could do everything we could think of,
haunted by our hope and faith and pity
and hate.

When they came in numbers we recoiled
but remembered the last sleeping place
of Heraclites, Aristotle, and Boneparte
the soup wagons of old wars.
We saw they could smile, their limbs
ready perpetually to do what we no longer
wanted—

sweep the night stars
for changeless meaning, the uncommon in each
breath and step begotten of each breath and step

Goya's *Two Old Ones Eating Soup*[*]
~ Sandra M. Gilbert

Beyond gender but not, no not beyond
appetite, these two at table loom
through a broth of black, the larger

still alert as if to greet & share
the salty swirls in the bowl
with an unknown guest, the other

bent to a mystifying text, bald skull pre-
occupied as a general might be if brooding
on the lines of combat.

     But the diner,
ah! the diner—with what a rictus of a grin this still
half-human wide-eyed creature gestures

toward the spoon that's just now dipping
into the soup. Any minute now that muck will rise
to the toothless mouth, any minute now the old one

will be swallowing it.

[*] *Viejos comiendo sopa.* Usually translated as "Two Old Men Eating Soup" but sometimes
interpreted as "two old women" or "two old witches."

For Miguel in Venice
~ Beckian Fritz Goldberg

The prism-necked pigeons follow you everywhere.
They sit puffed up like rainclouds beneath your table, one
on the seat of the chair across. Let him eye you. Whoever
you were somewhere else is a ghost. You
have returned to the old world, shadows stretched
in the late light, the sinking
palaces, the windows filled with water, the old world
at ease with death. Melon rinds bob carelessly
floating under the bridge, later, where you stop
to watch the moon scattered on the dark canal.
Only where the light falls can you see the water thinking.
I want to tell you a few nights ago
the cat brought me a dark gift in her mouth
and laid it down on the floor, still moving. It was
small as a man's thumb, a newborn rat with
closed eyes and a pink belly. When I nudged it
with a piece of cardboard, it flexed its toes,
lifted its arms. I shivered. I did not want to
touch him. The cat wanted to bat him around
for a while. We both had our primitive reasons.
I tell you just to let you know things
back here are sad and extraordinary. You
make out with the hairdresser, walk home
in the city's blackness and gloss, city like the wet dream
of Edgar Poe were he Italian. The hairdresser
follows you everywhere. When you turn around
he disappears. You can smell the water.
Along the edge the black-prowed gondolas tied up
jostle like horses. Everyone is asking
why you've stayed so long and when
you're coming back. But I say stay

if you want to. Die there. Who doesn't wish
dreams were money. Take the winged lions
and fly them off the golden dome of San Marco
and fuck anyone who says it can't be done.
Plenty can be done in beauty that can't be
in the world. Here the dry winter
has made me want to sleep, to burrow like the rabbits
under the cholla. I want to lie in bed and inhale
the clean sheets of my childhood. I want to rest
and hold on. But I was disturbed that night
by a life I didn't want. I bent down, slid the cardboard
under, stood up with the thing squirming on it, and
began to carry it somewhere—not outside
in the cold—somewhere. I laid him by the wall
next to the shelves in the garage. He lay on his side,
curled. We had two rat traps near the door.
They'd eaten papers in a storage box, left their scat.
Yet I looked down at that tiny thing
and got it in my head I needed to keep him warm
at least and came back with an old knitted cap
which he grasped at as I rolled him onto it
and folded it over him like an orange wool cave.
I knew he was going to die. You say
you've seen two rats in Venice, one running
by you the night you fell in love with the opera house.
You say everything was dripping with jewels—
Some afternoons you take the boat to the cemetery,
your namesake, San Michele. You like the view from there
looking back at the city, the single spruce charcoal
and blue smudge against the winter sky. We cannot
look at the world enough. Things here
are ridiculous and fragile. I mean Goddammit.
I couldn't sleep. How bewildering it must be

for a body, suddenly pushed into the wombless air,
blind, hairless, born dying for touch.
And hungry. So believe I went back into the garage
with a Q-tip dipped in milk and tried to swab
the baby rat's mouth which never opened. His body
stretched out so I saw his pink underside, his
delicate hands and feet which curled around
the stick and tried to hold it. This plague.
This filthmonger. This breath. Tell me
if I was stupid or just crazy and what I should have done.
Tell me how the hairdresser had some drawings
by Michaux and knew the French ambassador
who served you tea in his study wearing velvet slippers.
Life is wretched. You admit you'll come back
for your medicine, you miss your dog.
I'm never going anywhere again. I mean it.
I couldn't sleep. I couldn't go back in the garage.
I couldn't be the crazy woman growing old raising
her rat-child. It was cold out, but I stood there
for some time, the full moon a fairy gold
floating in the blackness which contained
all largeness, all intimacies, and smelled sweet
bittersweet like the creosote. We learn
to love beauty most for its disregard.

Nieces and Nephews
~ Marilyn Hacker

In July, when Tsahal was bombing Gaza
and we marched, and there were flags and brawls
Lamis waited for me on the corner, smiling
in a lime-green sleeveless dress, not her daily jeans.
There were three cop cars parked in front of my building
and Lamis shouted giddily in Arabic
"She's the terrorist, here!" I pinched her,
shushed her, laughing "Half those cops are Arabs!"
We went to a café, drank wine. She told me
her niece had finally been freed from prison
in Damascus. She lit up her cell phone
to show me the 19-year-old girl's photo.
The second of her older sister's children.

Naima's Ismaël on the Corniche, sunlit
in a rust corduroy jacket, white shirt open
at the neck, smiles next to his aunt in paisley
hijab and movie-star dark glasses.
Wind scuds the waves beyond. Out of Mosul
for the first time in his life, she, out of danger
for the first time in six months. The last
check-point, the last baksheesh, the abaya
shoved into a suitcase. A walk on Sunday,
a future open as the wine-dark sea.

I drank wine in the same café with Fadwa
last week, at midnight, talking about meters—
blank verse, alexandrines and al-mursal—
though she was keen to go outside and smoke
in the insidious slant winter rain.
"Have you heard from Lamis? I haven't seen her

in a month, she didn't answer an e-mail."
"Her nephew," said Fadwa, "died in prison
under torture." The first of those five children.

I'll meet Ismaël in Beirut with Naima.
In Beirut, no one arrests the daughters
or the nephews of the neighbors these days,
so she can bitch and moan about the neighbors
and how her students can't translate as-Sayyab
"Nothing but Iraq ..." The rain is falling
on all the suburbs where it lives in exile
and Lamis isn't answering the phone.

Ghost Guest
~ Rachel Hadas

I sometimes think I recognize the face
of my own death. Knowing it is nearer
makes me feel it ought to be familiar,
neutral guest I've seen somewhere before.
Even if it's not a face I know,
can it be ignored,
that shadow presence quiet in a corner?
And therefore as a stranger give it welcome.
Which is the lesser of two evils here,
which the least boorish way to be a host?
Who is hosting whom? If I'm a host,
I'm also just as much a guest, a ghost.
What heart heard of, ghost guessed. So,

Death, I'll acknowledge you, I'll be polite,
hand you a drink and let you circulate
and talk with others. You will cycle back.
Precisely: at my back I always hear
and do not hear and see and do not see,
know and do not know you'll catch up with me.
Since I think I know you from somewhere,
why should I be so sure
that you do not know me at least as well,
my length of days and my Achilles heel,
which in each person's in a different place?
Sometimes I think I recognize your face.

Swallows Escort Us From Village to Village in Crete
~ Barbara Hamby

They're like the neighborhood welcoming committee
    swooping down as we enter a little village
and seem to stay with our car until we drive away,
    and I can imagine their chatter: *Who was that?*
I thought it was Angelis at first, but he has a red car.
    Thank God they're gone. It's May, and Persephone
is in the world again, her mother gone mad with flowers—
    pink and white oleander and huge bushes of gold
along the winding roads. No one seems to know its name,
    though I ask every chance I get, and the drifts
of Queen Anne's Lace that seem to spread a false winter
    on every abandoned roadside in Siberia, Mississippi,
and now Crete, and I discover that it is *Daucus carota,*
    or wild carrot. Who knew the common orange tuber
had such a delirious hat? O those mysterious selves
    that dwell in every body—the farmer inside
the lawyer, the professor inside the fireman, the dancer
    inside the nurse. How can we name anything
when there are so many selves, like the Japanese *tatemae,*
    which means "outside face," the face you show
other people, the face that allows you to escort someone
    through an art gallery, show him your favorite view
of Kyoto, and then take him to a restaurant where you
    celebrated your thirtieth anniversary with your wife,
all the while loathing him. You are bolstered by *hone,*
    your inner thoughts for no matter how happy,
everyone must confront *sabi,* a severe loneliness,
    because at least we are born in the company
of a mother, but our exit is more iffy, so I am hoping
    for a company of swallows to lead me on
to that undiscovered country or maybe mockingbirds

because I will need a lecture or perhaps cardinals,
since there is a nest outside my bedroom window,
    and every morning they are there announcing
the new day with a cry of *birdie, birdie, birdie, birdie.*

We Miss The Boat To Gramvusa
~ Barbara Hamby

Because we take a less direct road, the romantic winding one
       with gorges and waterfalls, and like all romantic
decisions this one turns out to be three-quarters stupid
       and one quarter sublime, or is it the other way
around? No, at best it's half and half, but only for a few
       seconds in isolated moments like celestial
Technicolor commercials in a boring black and white movie,
       the movie being our lives, so the road is sepia toned
and covered in boulders from the mountain above
       because we are on the dry side of Crete now,
and the wildflowers are parched, there's no way we're
       going to make the last boat for the island rumored
to be the citadel of Aeolus, the king of the winds,
       one of Odysseus's stops, where he charmed
· the king with his stories, which seems to have been his super
       power, and as a reward was given a bag of the winds,
but his men think it's treasure and when they open the bag
       they are thrown off course, and isn't that a human
predicament? You have your map marked, your itinerary
       booked, your menu set, and then the weather
changes, a revolution erupts, the fish spoils, or the road
       is destroyed so we stop the car, walk around the signs,
look at the map, and then go back the way we came,
       and as we drive up to the dock in Kavonisi, we see
the boat rounding the head, so what to do but stop and order
       a beautiful lunch of fresh fish and salad,
which always elevates the mood, and I feed my scraps
       to a black tomcat with white boots and pink battle scars,
and think of my super power which is being able to wedge
       twice as many containers into my tiny freezer
than I should be able to, and look out at the sea,

which makes me feel romantic, in the sense
that Lord Byron was when he went left Italy to fight for the Greeks,
 so we head off to the dirt road on the peninsula,
and there are bee hives, and when we reach the road's end,
 there are donkeys, and the bees bombilate in the dittany
and wild grass, and we climb to a point and below is the beach of Balos,
 with water a glorious Technicolor blue, and in the distance
Gramvusa, where the King of the Winds maybe had his palace,
 and maybe Odysseus stopped there in his wooden ship
after escaping from Polyphemus, his heart still beating,
 not knowing where he was, only wanting to go home.

The Cabin People
~ Allison Adelle Hedge Coke

from Sissy

Twisting white over grey, ribbons
lash out in sharp winds,
out of stone chimney tops
from the log house.
That place so long without human company
ghosts moved in and about freely.
Suddenly, it appears those ghosts are not alone.

They must have come at night,
placing dried grass over gravel
to mute the crackle in the drive.

Blackbirds by the hundreds
circled and spiraled in swarms.
The winged cluster, shift and dark,
skipping up drafts, diving in and out,
up, down, over, through, and
around the entire valley border
the day before the ghosts showed themselves.

We watched them through
broken window panes and splintered logs,
through big round hay bales stacked so long
they looked like wooly mammoths.

They showed themselves.
Barefoot, bare-chested white boys
playing yard ball in the snow.

Their stiff blond hair and wobbly legs
belonged tucked away at school.
Not here, in this brown-skinned world
Not outside at five below freezing.

At night they vanished
as if they'd never appeared save
a faint burning behind drawn shades.
Cotton wicks and kerosene in glass
hung from rafters for light.
We squinted and gawked as long as we could
barely making out fuller figures,
shifting and turning like blackbirds warming to roost.

Three grown-up versions of the boys,
we invented histories for them all.
Not knowing if they were female or male
Not knowing where they came from and why.
We decided they were refugees
from the outside, from the enemy's world,
from their own modern society.
They became for us a pastime,
garbled gossip and pony dreams come real,

something to testify to the reservation appeal we all knew,
to the real necessity of log houses and stone chimneys
and junked cars no one could afford to fix up.
Something to chase monsters and ghosts with bad intent far away.
They became what we needed them to be.
Proof that even some of their own couldn't
make it in the white, white world.
We pitied them and thought of sharing fry bread.
We wondered how they escaped arrest for truancy.

The entire winter quarter, they eluded,
and we pursued.
One day, when the sky stayed the same strange pink and blue
it was all night before,
my niece discovered another child, a girl,
playing deep in snow and breaking ice
on a red pitcher pump.

She came home red-faced and told this story
in low whispers and with her stubby fingers cold as bones.
How the children had no names and
how, though we had never seen squatters before,
they had always lived this way.
The girl was older, maybe six or seven years,
(even she could not be sure)
she had been to school one time and learned so much geography
she gave the boys geographic names herself
(she'd grown so tired of Buddy and Brother).

The girl was fascinated by the Saint Lawrence River,
by Indianapolis and Chattanooga city.
So, Brother, Brother and Brother became
Lawrence, Indiana, and Tennessee.
Though they all still called her Sissy, she called herself
Sault Ste. Marie.
My niece was the gurgle of the creek
her eyes shining obsidian stone.
We listened to her reveling
and gathered courage sliding out between our toes.

"Zat so." said old Grandma.
Dey ain't hurt nobody.

Maybe day like us, just want to be left alone.
Maybe we should leave 'em that way."
And that's exactly what we do.
They've been on the rez about eighteen months,
the boys still got no shoes.

We like to stay up late at night
with coffee thick as horse glue,
and make up stories for them, one by one,
each one's got something new.
They become what we need them just then,
outlaws or refugees,
they're like our own private little side show.

Like we were to Billy Cody.
The stranger whites among the Skins.
The gist of mystery.
Old Grandma with her puckered face,
crepe-papered skin, sympathetic heart,
she spared those loathsome white folks
but, late at night, in the wildest tales

we still rip them all apart.

The Other One
~ John Hennessy

Straight man in short-shorts, man-flats, eyeliner. Cap-gun
guitar, white blouse. Blow-drier. Skippingly circling
endlessly. Always behind or beside, the same again—
not quite. Never up front, never the Greek but working
on it, more Tiber, near Nile, pop-Alexandrian.
The plainly less pretty, less talented one. The black-eyed,
hesitant, not-George-Michael, nose-jobbed son.
(Club-jumped, their manager claimed, tough-guyed. He lied.)
Old what's his name. Surprised some to learn he had one.
He played at guitar. Propped out. *Andrew Ridgeley*—
I looked it up—flopped solo, crashed race cars, didn't he?
Joke-butt, most likely to be forgotten, still fun
to make fun of. Partnered *up*, though, Bananarama's Keren—
years, now. Surfed off, Cornwall sets. Went Green! Impressed *me*.

Zipf's law: a love poem
~ Bob Hicok

"The of, and to a in
is I, that it for you
was with on, as have,
but be they"[1]

in order of word frequency,
are the most common words
hidden inside everything you and I
have ever written—love notes,
bomb threats, novels

even weirder fun: in writing
these words more than we've written
all others, we've penned the
twice as often as of, three times and,
and for every to, scribbled or typed
four thes, etcetera, down
to the twenty-to-one ratio
of the to they, because, it seems,
we're human

two things we do—simplify
and repeat, repeat

a third—make love
where horses ran, ran, run

a fourth—adore secrets

I, that this collective poem

---

1 Linebreaks mine.

calmly sleeps within the churn
of our differences, verse
that obviously needs work—more verbs
than grabby have and snoozy be
would be exciting, and at least
one noun such as coatrack
to stand up or stick around—
but there it is, the infrastructure
of all our flutterings to amuse,
confuse and arouse each other

statistically, I'm mystically inclined
to think it means we're even closer
than our orgies suggest, since our lips
touch so often, share so much
common ground in sound,
and find it Romantic that a nerd
with the un-sexy name of Zipf
figured this out and wasn't too shy
to tell us a wave braids through everything
we—who are so much water,
mostly oceans in blue jeans—say

even languages we can't translate
show this pattern
of word frequency, which is freaky
but geeks me more than makes me fret
our predictability, I see it
as marvel, how there's always something
under bones and sky holding us up,
three cheers for buoyancy

a fifth thing we do—want to fly

Save The Children
~ Tony Hoagland

I regret to bring up the subject, but it's time to stop making kids. The
    cities are filled up with people who keep making more

of each other, who keep making garbage, and keep not hauling it away.
That noise in the streets?
It's to drown out the sound of extinction.

Oh, children of the future!—already I can feel them assembling their
    courtrooms and juries
for staging the war crime tribunals

that will hold us responsible
for the blight of their inheritance, the earth—
& I don't believe I can bear
the death of the trees and the birds and the seas.

For that reason I wish to propose a solution— that the children be held
in protective custody
in the country of birth control.

Now that the ascent of progress has stopped,
now that the erection of empire has become dysfunctional
-now that god has pulled the ejection lever,
and our time is about to become, as they say, biblical,

the great blue angel of Planned Parenthood has paid me a visit,
and spread her wings in my heart
and instructed me to make the announcement:

Yo, all you dudes and ladies! You home-girls and low-riding squires!
    You tattooed Shannons and spider-limbed Malenas:

Let us rescue the kids
by simply forgoing their creation.

Fornicate freely— but hold your fire!
Be as hot as you want— but aim to the side! Don your prophylactic
    couture before tangos.
Put on your fireman suits; install your uterine umbrellas.

Shut up the holes, for the babies!
The silence you hear will be the sound of no one saying Thank you,
and then, like applause, coming back,
the honest, respectful response: the sound of
No one, saying You're welcome.

Days of 2015
~ Michael Hofmann

Money is speech. Firms have feelings. The People's Republic of Facebook
is offended by that woman's pseudonym,
takes a copy of her passport to have her account made out to her real
    identity.

Your bank card is good for drawing cash, but
not for a balance or a statement. The Greeks, meanwhile,
revert to barter. One wolf cries "terrorist!"

and sheep come from miles around to applaud a (Kurdish) boy being
    savaged.
(It's called NATO.) A list of NSA search terms
is so confidential, it can be shown to one person, if that.

Beate Zschäpe, on trial for the past two years for her part
in the racial murder of ten people, shares giggles
with her latest defense lawyer (28), cold-shoulders

the other three. The accused bench is like a box at the opera,
there she is, popping a cachou into the new boy's mouth, cynosure,
    flash of cleavage.
Wagner directs Wagner. Disparities widen; "scissors" is the German
    term of art.

Cities fill up / empty out (your choice) with "buy to leave" property.
Countries not busily pursuing their dissolution (UK, Belgium) harden
    themselves.
Walls go up against Serbia, Mexico, Palestine. A large body of water
    (Australia) is of course ideal.

Donald Trump pioneers the quick-drying comb-under.

The Republicans come up this time with sixteen (digit sum: seven) dwarves.
Never mind the quality, feel the narrowness.

The weather breaks records every which way; traffic reports—
miles of *Stau*—go on forever. Railways lose money hand over fist, but
    continue
their policy of neurotically expressive pricing (no two the same).

The Chinese stock exchange gets all kittenish at a cost of trillions.
America is good for an atrocity a week ("gun violence"), and doesn't get it.
Brazenness or apology: a style choice. Putin is a figure from Artaud or
    Genet;

"Sepp" Blatter wins and flounces out of FIFA, postdated; "el Chapo"
burrows out of a high-security Mexican prison on a rail-mounted
    motorbike.
Lame-duck Obama goes to Africa to preach the virtues of term limits.

Human rights lawyers disappear like old snow or coral reefs or old-
    growth forests.
Most constitutional arrangements are subject to review,
most trade is with China. Nothing trumps (trumps!) immediate
    gratification.

Governments continue to attempt to refine their populations.
The new instrument of domestic policy is the F-16,
used by Syria, and now, three years later, by Turkey as well.

Saudi Arabia apes the US; a "loose" alliance "of the willing" bombs
    Yemen every day for months.
Whole families up sticks and emigrate to ISIS, if they can find it,
    or, failing that, ISIL.
Religions have feelings. Cartoons aren't funny. Speech costs.

Willow
~ T. R. Hummer

Sometimes the willow is immutable, and I don't know why,
    any more than I know why darkness travels
From midnight to midnight faster than thought. I spend
    part of every morning saying *I don't know* to the geranium
And part saying *I can't say* to the cat sleeping by the door.
    I'm trying to make up for the times I cannot bring myself
To admit my ignorance and I keep on talking, when the quarrel
    will not stop itself in my larynx. *Oh foolish language,*
Just be still, someone might beg, but it keeps on running
    like a cement mixer on steroids. You might as well say
Begone to the whirlwind, or will the garbage truck in the alley
    not to exist. The Logos gets me by the throat, the riptide
Of its endless sentence contradicting absence, cancelling silence,
    dragging me down forever into the vortex of utterance.
It wants to outline how the blood cells flicker in sexual patterns,
    It wants to parse how the neutrino knows its nest.
I stand on the stump of the willow at high noon on a Tuesday,
    letting discourse immerse me. Even the dead are helpless
In its corrosive current. They keep muttering over and over,
    Bring us a bowl of goat's blood so we can suck it down
And argue. It's tradition. And if I mourn a little for the tree
    that shaded me even before sunrise, it goes on living surely
In the brackish plasma where the syllables hyphenate and breed.

A Zipper
~ Mark Irwin

In an hour the stars still loading will swarm
like seconds found, and something

about stars was a song he lulled
us to sleep with, fifty years ago. *Ago*, the second half of that word
streaming into the *what*

was I fish back—silver and shaking now—or perhaps later at a red

light, as part of the streaming traffic
pauses, and for a moment those notes

flesh the present like migrant sand on a name chiseled

in stone. Sometimes
the margins of our lives seem unbearable, a zipper

against the dark we tear

open toward a gleam that briefly
devours. Recalling

that song I can almost fall asleep again, sleep in a steeper
sleep that moves like wind lifting a dried moth's wings.

Urban Renewal
~ Major Jackson

XXVII. Washington Square Park
for David & Stacey

When all that cautions the eyes toward the imminent
slide of autumn to arctic winds, the canopy of English elm
and sycamore leaves like colored coins fall and widen
a hole letting more light spill in, heaven's alms
to earth whose ashen gray and white will soon be all the rage,
and our guilty secret is the baby grand playing Glass's *Orphée*
Suite for Piano. Nearby Butoh dancers writhe & almost upstage
with white-painted faces of horror (portraits of Nagasaki?),
and past the fountain's water plumes, a drugged-riddled couple
share the smoldering remain of an *American Spirit*,
their grizzled dog roped to a shopping cart and frayed duffle
bag, this city's updated scene of the *American Gothic*.
Our reddish-haired pianist lets the melancholic notes
float to high-rise buildings on Fifth above its triumphal arch,
like a film in reverse where the golden foliage is read by a poet
as autumn's light pours in. "Don't Get Around Much
Anymore," The Ink Spots version on Decca spins on
a phonograph, an era spiraling softly then held by a gentle wind.

End of Summer
~ Mark Jarman

    seemed impossible.
How could there be an end to summer?
Boys and girls with blond sand on our brown necks,
when school clamped down in August, we protested,
"But it's still summer!"
          But it wasn't.
The sun still burning, the waves still breaking,
summer always ended before it ended.
   "It's not as hot this year as other summers, is it?"
she wrote as we were leaving one another.

Summer, a country like a floating memory,
the good place you can wear upon your skin
like a lace of salt or the name of one you loved.
And fall and spring and winter, for that matter.

Dying, asked which was her favorite season,
the woman who'd been born in the height of summer
looked at the window where the leaves were turning,
and answered, "All of them."

Kameraden
~ Krzysztof Jaworski

Rzuciłem ziemię skąd mój ród, co do mowy
to też, ani me
ani be. Pokazali mi
muzeum, pokazali mi kościół.
Nie chodziłem pijany,
nie kradłem po sklepach.
Wszyscy tam mieli mnie chyba
za chorego umysłowo?
To bardzo piękny kraj, może
i dorobiłbym się na czyszczeniu wychodków, może nawet
powstałby z tego jakiś nowy kierunek
w sztuce (jestem
utajonym przywódcą duchowym swego pokolenia).
—Jesteś chyba jedynym Polakiem,
który przywiózł tu pieniądze,
żeby je wydawać, zaśmiał się.
Sam jest bez pracy—
nie chce dorobić się
na czyszczeniu wychodków, a sztukę
ma w dupie.
Myślę, że się lubiliśmy zanim wyjechał.
Gdyby był luty czterdziestego trzeciego, myślałbym o tym
czy Niemcy zdobędą Stalingrad.
Jest znacznie później.
Czekanie nie ma sensu.

Kameraden
~ Krzysztof Jaworski, translated by Benjamin Paloff

I abandoned the land of my tribe, and as for my speech,
that too, neither here
nor there. They showed me
the museum, they showed me the church.
I didn't walk around drunk,
I didn't steal from the stores.
Maybe they all took me
for sick in the head?
It's a very beautiful country, perhaps
I could even make a fortune cleaning latrines, it might even
give rise to some new movement
in art (I am
the secret spiritual leader of my generation).
"You may be the only Pole
who has brought money here
to give it away," he laughed.
He's without work as well:
he doesn't want to make a fortune
cleaning latrines, and as for art,
art can suck it.
I think we hit it off before he went away.
If it were February '43, I'd be thinking about whether
the Germans will take Stalingrad.
It's considerably later.
No point in waiting.

Early
~ Amanda Johnston

after Sharon Olds

I wrap you in morning water
smooth lotion over your legs
make you glisten like dew

I button your shirt, press
your collar down with my palm
kiss your forehead—wet amulet

I worry more than pray, call
to empty hands, let evening
return you unharmed if not holy

~ Pierre Joris

Another dawn's

sharp cat edge
perched on
balcony overlooks an
overgrown garden
overseen by
a veiled moon.
the air has water
in it. I add
smoke. the pink
of my heart
is not the pink
of the horizon.
en face: orange
clinker built
siding with
oval church
window built
in:
2 palm fronds
& what looks like
an abstract rose.
Which is what
morning is:
an abstract rose
keeps rising.

Ode to Disappointment
~ Marilyn Kallet

"Dear Marilyn,
The committee has decided
not to fund your Professional Development
proposal. We think you are already developed.
Other applications have risen to the top,
like chicken fat on cooling soup.
Other applicants may be newer,
less developed, but more promising,
more professional. Poetry
is not professional. Poetry sits alone in a dark
room and who knows what it does?
We suspect it touches itself.
You don't need a grant to write poetry.
All you need is a pen and a bottle.
Cheap swill. Think Bukowski,
We never offered him a dime.
Or Keats. We did not fund him. He mined his own
sources. You can find your own cash. Your husband,
for example, got the best raise ever this year,
because he scares us. We don't mean he's violent,
just that he never shuts up and his criticisms
are professionally developed. So go home and
sleep with your rich dick, we mean your spouse.
See how that works out. We have faith in your
ability to surmount us."

Aulos
~ Dore Kiesselbach

—an ancient Greek wind instrument that accompanied choral singing

Was it the guidebook or did you see it in passing and say stop?
We were headed south, for Sparta, but pulled the car
over, walked down into it, looked back at grass-softened
layers of stone from the direction the actors would have.
Our faces were petals pushed by the wind. For what earthly
purpose did we seek lineaments of bone—or was it only
me? Greece had been my vote for the best way to spend
your mother's miraculous trip fund. I'd been reading
Herodotus in a roachy residential hotel when her letter arrived.
Would knowing they applied bright paint to the Parthenon
have changed our destination? You were interested in where
the audience would have looked when the action turned
their eyes away. With terraces they made farms of hills,
shoulder upon shoulder holding the sky up like a flaming
bier. In the tiny top plot it was customary to plant a flowering
tree and water it religiously when the crops failed, which
we forgot to do or which ate shit on my shift. I claim
nothing of the scenes that followed save a blade of grass.
By thumbs held out of character it could have been a reed.

Creepy
~ John Kinsella

Who's to say someone else wouldn't have found it soothing—
the van across the narrow grass-spined road, engine running,

driver with cap rolling a cigarette—setting the paper, resetting
the paper, pouring tobacco back into pouch and doing

it over again? Or the house for sale with the buzzing
of an alarm somewhere deep inside, a bleak day tuning

itself to the range and the sea and the dank ground glowering
in between. A pheasant rises and crosses the road flapping

more than need be, furze is in riotous yellow but flowering
nowhere else nearby—just down low, with cows wintering

out while everywhere else in their sheds, and music playing
somewhere—a tune on which you can't get a grip. Can't sing

along with what doesn't go anywhere. And a massive dwelling
without a roof—crenulated mockery of clan-keeps on jutting

headlands, a folly of the boom when here was the rites of spring
even at the dead time of year. And passing muddy gateways, who's saying

it's not a wonderland? But as the van comes up slowly—following
me?—I find it hard to turn around, and when I do, I start running

for a place to step aside on this bent straight and narrow, fling
looks as he crawls by, fag in his mouth, and finger arcing

back and forth—a windscreen wiper. No No No settling
here son, keep moving, moving on. Suspicion is machinery belching

over the rise, a quarrying into the bloody stone of the range. Wanting
connection, I think of how strangers would take my comings

and goings over Jam Tree Gully into their estimations of belonging.
Startled by a pair of linnets, the male still with its red summering

feathers, I wonder if it's the warmth after storms that is creeping
me out. All this adjusting we're having to do. Ironising

is like the rhythm of the march to keep you going.
Walking a new road is always creepy—sediment clings.

The Purple Scrode
~ David Kirby

Whenever somebody talks about someone with excess
      body hair or a foot fetish or a lump on his forehead
that may or may not be a third eye, you can always
      get a laugh if you say, I went to high school with a guy
like that. And should someone ever say, Have you
      ever heard of climacophilia, that is, the erotic compulsion

to tumble down stairs, you'll have your audience
      in stitches if you simply say, Yeah, there was a guy
like that in senior biology lab. Why, though? Because
      high school is the last stop on the train to normalcy,
to the depot where we'll be sorted and sent to live
      with our own kind, with the ones who are go to work

and come home and do the dishes and pay the bills.
      Oh, a few loonies make it through to college, but they
seldom make it past freshman year. In my dorm,
      there was Pop Tart, who gave toaster pastries to anyone
he thought needed cheering up, whether they did
      or not. There was the girl on the floor below who

woke up with two broken ankles and no memory
      of how that had happened, and the one who got
dressed in her closet and ironed her bras. There was
      also a girl who was a witch, not as in "mean jerk"
but a real witch from a very nice witch family;
      she's one of the few who actually graduated

and is a cardiologist these days though still a witch.
      Then there was the Purple Scrode, who mainly decorated
every blank surface with Purple Scrode graffiti, though

sometimes late at night he would appear at the end
of the hall in his hoodie, spread his arms, cry
        "The Purple Scrode!" and take off with the rest of us

in hot pursuit. We never caught him, and his identity
        remains a mystery to this day. No one knew what
a scrode was, though it sounded anatomical, nor why
        it was purple, though we had our guesses as to that as well.
And then we grew up, moved on, got jobs, became wives
        and husbands, moms and dads. The Purple Scrode

is probably raising scrodes of his own now,
        though their names are Peter and James and Bethany.
They'll go to high school soon, and then what will
        happen to them? Something wonderful, I know.
Something they don't expect any more than you or I
        expected we'd be sitting here like this, thinking how

lucky we are that our schooling is behind us, that
        everything it promised came true, not in home room
or the gym or the cafeteria or biology lab or in the work
        that came after, the barbecues, the lazy family vacations
in the mountains or on the shore—nowhere in this sunny
        vitamin-enriched world, in fact, but in that forest

of the heart where we walk alone as others drop off
        their dry cleaning or pick up two avocados and wonder
which is riper or edge the sidewalk or call the meeting
        to order or dismiss it, and there we are, trying to see
as best we can in the darkness as owls and bats wheel
        through the trees, and at the edge of that forest, a wolf.

Love for Murder
~ Karl Kirchwey

I was sifting earth for our shade garden,
    maidenhair, aconite and sad hellebore,
      when a handful of dinosaurian nightmare
fell onto the brick patio's chevron

right beside me, ruffled and quivering
    like something out of Hieronymus Bosch,
      coal-black, sprinkled with white dots,
fired green and purple by the morning,

and in a silence so deep it felt satiric,
    lay there. Something territorial,
      I was sure, some ancient quarrel
I had better avoid, one starling's beak

curved on the other's breast in mastery,
    a cruel inwrought emblem,
      the wing trailing helplessly, the eyes' gleam.
But then onto a high branch of the catalpa

that would dangle its long seed pods in summer
    above the underworld of my weak surmise,
      I saw this fused thing flutter and rise:
for I had mistaken love for murder.

Waiting For An Apparition
~ Lance Larsen

Three hours I walked Père Lachaise, Paris's most famous cemetery, but kissed no one. No kiss for Colette or Edith Piaf. No Madeleine kisses for Proust, no white-gloved kisses in an invisible box for Marcel Marceau. Is a thrush a kiss? How about a seagull grubbing at bread crusts? No grace note kisses for Chopin, no lizard-man kisses for Jim Morrison. Who wants to *break on through to the other side* anyway? Is a flower dirty to its hips a kiss? Is sunlight on a drizzly morning a kiss from on high? No kisses for Richard Wright's rage, though his vault was at shoulder level. Did I kiss my wife during those three hours? I ate a drippy pear: let's count that as sublimation. No silk, over-the-shoulder kisses for Isadora Duncan. No pointillist kisses for Seurat. I could have kissed all the dead: I had that kind of map. At Oscar Wilde's tomb, with no warning, lipstick kisses everywhere: ten thousand *I do*'s, ten thousand shades of *I love you*, with leftover lip smacks extending to the lucky no-name sod next door, who took all devotional bursts full on the face. A gravestone is not a kiss, a kiss is not resurrection, though it's fun to practice. Meanwhile I found a note penned on a receipt, like a Chinese fortune: "I'm waiting for an apparition." Aren't we all? I'm slouchy in spirit, but tall when I stretch my shoulders. I kissed high to lessen the risk of contagion. I did not kiss in orange or magenta or watermelon frost, just dry American lips on stone. Farewell, hello, vertical reach, bragging rights, a little rain. Next an Italian teenager took her turn. After smooching the granite, she painted her father's mouth blood red and edged back, like a mother watching her son take his first drink.

Not to Be Expected
~ Sydney Lea

One evening before Youth Fellowship I found
Some organ pipes on the floor, and knelt beside them,
Singing "Long Tall Sally" into one. Meanwhile,
I signed my name with a finger in the dust
Of the nubbled concrete. No one had ever done
These things all at once—and no one ever would.
That was a fusty basement room in St. Luke's.

Why this recollection on the bank of a brook?
Less strange to remember a poem by Robert Frost,
Whose brook runs out of song and speed come June.
The one I'm standing beside has never sung,
Not ever run. It barely crawls at ice-out,
And by now, mid-May, its water's seeped to nothing.
What's new? Not much. It does this every year.

Snow melts, the freshets feed it, then it dies.
The barn opposed across the way … Enough
Of Frost, irrelevant here, where a barn is crumbling
In that field of weeds. It needs refurbishment,
Which it won't get. The sills are rotted, walls
All splayed like a doomed doe's legs on ice.
Did someone stand on its earthen ramp with a golf club?

Unlikely. Then how on earth did that dimpled ball,
Egg-like below me, land in its nest of dried algae?
Nothing's to be expected, never was.
Consider any two people, supposedly normal,
And prepare yourself to hear of odd behavior.
One may raise chinchillas, one love tango.
We wonder, *Who'd expect it?* Answer: no one.

I labored to be unique when I was young,
But what of my uncle, who'd listen to the *Ring*
Of the Niebelung while plucking his geese for the larder?
It was just what he did, not striving to be eccentric.
His brother, my father, served a tough stint as a soldier,
Regular army, Europe, World War II.
So why did he love to sing old navy tunes?

Search me. Search him. He hated all salt water.
I smell his bay rum now as I recall him,
And contemplate a ball in withered muck,
And note a certain barn, gap-toothed, neglected,
And conjure Robert Frost, a favorite author,
And remember an uncle, a basement, Little Richard—
Now what, I ask you, what can be expected?

X-Radiograph
~ Phillis Levin

Massacre of the Innocents, Pieter Bruegel the Elder

A woman is bending over
Something in the snow: it appears
To be an array of ham and cheese.
What is it doing there? Is she lifting her arms
In dismay, or uttering a prayer of gratitude?
Will the bounty be taken away
By the soldiers closing in, or has abundance
Fallen unbidden
From a bitter winter sky?

According to the X-ray, the winter
Is just as bitter
But there is no ham, no cheese, though that
Is what the naked eye sees.
It isn't hunger, it's not a day of plunder,
Something else is bringing her to her knees.
If you look a little closer, the shadow
Of an infant shows through: you can find
Many such shadows in the scene.

A soldier is herding women to a doorway,
Armored knights on stallions
Stand guard. At another door is a soldier
Seizing a child who hasn't been painted over
(Changed into a bundle or a loaf of bread).
A dog is barking, birds have fled,
Icicles hang from the eaves,
By a frozen pond a riderless horse
Rubs its head on a tree.

Over another bundle (another infant
Shadow) another woman grieves.

For a couple imploring a soldier
To spare a pale winged creature almost
As big as the daughter, whose father
Is pointing to her, read: "Take the girl,
Instead of our baby son" (concealed
Under a goose—or is it a swan?—
About to have its neck slashed open).
A soldier pissing against a wall
Disguises nothing at all.

Men bearing lances spear a rooster,
Stabbing until the last of the flock is dead.
Women faint at the sight of a dying boar
(A boy newly born not long before).
A woman cradles a pitcher: if the man
Hovering near her seems thirsty,
Do not fear: he will not spill any water,
The pitcher isn't a pitcher, the deed
He must do has been done.

The plunder has begun: it is bringing
Various people to their knees.
That is what a naked eye
Sees (a mother and child in flight
Were partially lost when another side
Of the panel was cut down).
As for the faded pair of socks
In the snow, they are
A faded pair of socks in the snow.

NOTE:

When Pieter Bruegel the Elder painted *Massacre of the Innocents* (circa 1565–1567), he gave the story in St. Matthew's Gospel a contemporary context. X-radiography reveals that the scene originally depicted Spanish troops and their German mercenaries killing the children of a Flemish village; by 1621 the canvas had been altered to suggest an act of plunder, with animals and household objects concealing the infants underneath. The painting's first known owner, Rudolf II Habsburg, King of Hungary and Bohemia, and Holy Roman Emperor, was probably responsible for having the painting altered. The painting was acquired by Charles II in 1662 and is in the Royal Collection, the King's Dressing Room, Windsor Castle.

Tendril
~ Phillis Levin

Incandescent coil,
Light by which we read the light

Spiraling through you—

Nimble filament, by touch
Renewed, by touch commencing.

Muir Woods

Meet Me Under the Whale
~ Timothy Liu

I don't remember what hour
it was we met, only that

the room was hot. I don't

remember if there was even
a clock in the room, only

that you had stolen the hands

off its face, eyes already
darting under the table—slips

of the tongue like paper cuts

we would get to suck on
while a chanteuse nonchalantly

took the stage. You looked

at me like a worm crawling
on a glass globe, waiting

for something to come along

and pluck you off. Seems
like we'd been ordering

off the same menus for years

only the prices had changed—

note for note, the songs

no longer recognizable

as we rode into the mouth
of a whale full of untold

myths, staircases spiraling

down. It hardly matters now
who asked for the check

or even who paid, how much

everyone got tipped. We
were in there for a long time

trying to decide—*Master*

the Tempest is Raging
tinged with its laissez-faire

jazz while our lady leaned on

a baby grand, her combs
inlaid with mother of pearl

thrown down—bleached bones

and tongues of the damned
washing up on shore

in the corners of our eyes.

Autoportret Në Tekstil
~ Luljeta Lleshanaku

Jeta ime është kjo garderobë veshjesh
e zgjedhur me sy dhe rrallëherë më prekje.

Kjo këmishë mendafshi e paveshur kurrë
prêt për një xhaketë mashkullore në supe,
që të mbyllë ciklin e saj floreal.
Kur s'ka ardhur, nuk do të vijë! Hidhe pa frikë!

Kjo bluzë dekolte akriliku
kombinohet me një buzëqeshje dy herë më të madhe se unë,
dhe një smalt të përkryer. Vite më parë ishte e kundërta.
Hidhe, as kjo nuk të bën punë.

Kurse ky fustan, të vetmen herë u vesh në një mbrëmje romantike.
Herën tjetër, nëse ka një të tillë,
deti të hedh në ishull pas dymijë vjetësh,
e deri atëherë, do t'i ketë kaluar moda.
Hidhe, zë vendin kot.

Kjo triko e bardhë është nostagji për të shkuarën; bluja-për të ardhmen
të dyja thithin oksigjenin e dhomës gjatë natës. Hidhi!

Kjo xhaketë e zezë kadifeje, është blerë me të lirë
tek mallrat e përdorur. Mbaje!
Është gjithmonë më lehtë të fshihesh pas lëkurës së tjetrit.

Kjo këmishë ekscentrike me vija bardhë e zi
është një alibi për t'u ndodhur në dy vende njëkohësisht.
Mbaje! Është vonë për të ndërruar stil!

Kjo pallto e rëndë si mjegulla kontinentale
dy numra më të mëdhenj, e blerë shtrenjtë dhe me nxitim për raste
    ceremoniale,
u var vetëm në korridore. Jam në borxh me të; lërë të rrijë!

Këto këpucë shik me taka ta larta
nuk e kanë instiktin e kthimit. Hidhi!
Hidhi dhe këto cizme elegante që të sollën fat të keq
që herën e parë. Kanë të drejtë marinarët kur thonë:
"Kur merr rrugë të panjohura, mos vish këpucë të reja!"

Ja dhe veshjet gri, të preferuarat e mia, njëra pas tjetrës …
Pa to, jam si qeni me jargët jashtë!
Të vjetra, por, mbaji!

Dhe këtë shall me dhjetëra variacione ngjyrash si qytete të nxehta
    kaotike.
ma dhuroi dikush, i cili, përmes meje,
donte të dilte prej radiografisë së vet. Hidhe; nuk ke vend për të!
Dhe kjo cantë e vockël, që zë fare pak gjëra:
një shami, një kuti pomadë për thembrat dhe një numër telefoni.
Mbaje, është alteregoja ende e papërdorur
do t'i vijë shumë shpejt koha!

Po e kuqja; c'do kjo pulovër e kuqe në raftin tim?!!!
Përcarëse, në shkak dhe pasojë. Hidhe; cfarë prêt?!
Dhe më në fund, veshjet e përditshme, të rehatshme,
që nuk të lënë kurrë në baltë dhe që nuk kanë nevojë as për hekur.
Një seri kompromisesh që kanë marrë formën time të trupit.
Mbaji; nuk je e lirë t'i hedhësh!

Në dysheme, hedhurinat avullojnë si një mitër gjigande
gjithë fantazinë e dështuar të një gruaje,

E ato pak pak gjëra që mbetën,
mund të lëvizin lirshëm në raft bërrylat më në fund,
si gondolierët, një një rrip të përsosur uji.

Dhe unë që prej vitesh s'e kisha kuptuar
nëse ngushëllohej apo shfajësohej ime më,
kur mërmëriste me zë: "Është stof safi, i qepur me dorë",

sa herë që pastronte me pak benzinë kostumin e saj të vetëm.

Self-Portrait in Woven Fabric
~ Luljeta Lleshanaku, translated by Ani Gjika

My life is a wardrobe—
clothes picked out with a quick glance
hardly ever with a touch.

This never-worn silk shirt
wants a man's jacket over its shoulders,
to end the blooming cycle.
Since it hasn't yet arrived, it never will.
Throw it away, don't think twice!

This décolleté acrylic blouse
matches a smile twice my size
and the impeccable enamel of front teeth.
Years ago, the opposite was true.
Toss it, it's useless.

And this dress, worn only once to a romantic dinner.
Next time, if there's another love like this, in another thousand years,
you're more likely to be cast away on an island by the sea,
and by then, the dress will be out of fashion anyway.
Dump it, it's just taking up space.

This white cardigan is pure nostalgia for the past; the blue one—for
    the future.
They suck the oxygen out of the room at night. Away with them both!

This black corduroy jacket, a cheapo
from a second hand store. Keep it!
It's always easier to hide behind someone else's skin.

This eccentric shirt with its black and white lines—
an alibi for finding yourself in two places at once.
Keep it! Too late to change your style!

This coat, heavy like inland fog
two sizes too big, too expensive, bought in a hurry for a ceremony,
hung only in hallways. I'm still paying for it; let it be!

These classic high-heel shoes
just have no instinct of return. Out they go!
Throw away even these fine boots; they only brought you bad luck
from the start. Sailors are right when they say:
"Don't put on new shoes when crossing unknown seas!"

And here are the gray clothes, my favorites, one after the other …
Without them, I'm exposed, like a drooling dog!
They're old, but keep them anyway!

And this scarf with many colors like humid, chaotic cities.
A gift from someone who, by giving it to me,
hoped to fill the x-ray film of his life,
his impenetrable bones.
Throw it! There's no space for it!

And this small purse where nearly nothing fits:
a handkerchief, a tube of foot cream, a phone number.
Keep it—a spare alter ego,
it could come in handy.

And red; what's a red sweater doing in my drawer,
looking for a fight?
Throw it; what are you waiting for?

And finally, wrinkle-free, everyday
comfortable clothes that never disappoint.
A string of compromises that have taken the shape of my body.
Keep them, you're not allowed to toss these!

On the floor, the discarded clothes evaporate like a gigantic womb
that miscarried a woman's entire fantasy.
And the few items left
can finally move their elbows freely in the dresser
like gondoliers on a perfect strip of water.

And as for me, for years I hadn't understood
if my mother was commiserating or making excuses
when she'd mumble: "It's pure wool, hand-made,"
each time she'd clean her only suit with a few drops of gasoline.

Britain, Dawn
~ William Logan

Morning's palette of ash.
The dawn local squeezes through brownfields
burnished with postmodern architecture,
abrupt prefab cartoons.

The woody stalks lurking along the tracks,
Reverend Buddle's contribution to Linnaean order,
wait like adolescents to burst into bloom—
late invaders, ridiculous, almost unkillable.

Were these dyed-in-the-wool purply curiosities,
Caribbean visitors not anxious to return,
the souls such artless buildings were looking for
or had inconveniently misplaced?

The Barber Shop
~ William Logan

The reek of hair oil, tobacco, and shaved necks,
scissors marinating in blue Barbicide,
as if there barbers went to drown.

Bolted to the side of the shop,
the red-and-white pole turned, turned.
There were two chairs in Jack Jeans' Barber Shop.

Jeans bossed the oldest, chrome
and brick-red oilcloth, the horsehair seat
with a New Bedford phonebook to prop me up.

Ragged magazines slumped beside the waiting benches,
the cooler of Coke and Cliquot Club.
The retired warriors of Troy yarned the day away.

Those Saturday morning rituals
ended when Mother bought a pair of electric clippers.
First she shaved the left side of my head,

then the right, the left again,
then she called Jack Jeans.
After hours, he did what could be done.

There I knew the emptiness of small towns.

The Dishwasher
~ James Longenbach

For many years I saved my money, bought a car, a new car, a Chevette.
Lean on me, said the radio, *when you're not strong*.

I'd known that song since I was young but every time I heard it
I wanted to hear it again.
I drove to the supermarket, then drove home.
I looked in the refrigerator, under the bed.

As if I were standing in the kitchen, unloading the dishwasher,
    holding the phone,
I heard my mother's voice.
I heard it plainly, as if she were standing in the room.

I know it's early, she said,
But I'm planning ahead for Christmas.

So I'd like to remember: what kind of coffee do you like?
Regular, or decaf, or both at certain times?
I want to be prepared, in case you'd like a cup when you're here.

Age Of Innocence
~ James Longenbach

Thirty years ago, in a Burger King on Mount Hope Avenue,
There was a fly. Preferably

I'd be writing in the present tense,
Lurching forward unpredictably, but with pleasure.

After you're dead, you can choose the way you write; my mother told
    me so.

Twice the fly buzzed, three
Times, then settled on my hand.

Manure Pile Covered in Snow
~ Thomas Lux

When the horses' heads got too close to the beams above,
and they pinned back their ears each time they saw me,
I had no choice
but to lay wide barn boards
on the four feet of snow
for thirty yards or so
from the stalls to the top of the pile.
Load a wheelbarrow—I favored a pitchfork first,
next the shovel. Then get a running start
on the downslope board
from the stable door,
rush it to the pile's top, and flip
both handles with a hard twist.
It was labor—and my father said
to do it—to be done.
Aesthetics? I had none.
So: I ruined a pristine mound
of snow. A mound so symmetrical, so round,
it seemed a Half-Sphere from the Spheres,
or perhaps a sky god's giant tear
fallen and frozen, smothered by white.
And I soiled it, tossing one barrowload left,
the next right, over and over. After each run,
I carved on the stable door: 1,
then 1, then 1, and one more,
then crossed all four.
And started another. I worked hard
until the horses stood level again
in their stalls, and accepted extra oats.
They were shaggy in their winter coats.

It never snowed again that year,
and not near to four feet since.

Mr. True
~ Maurice Manning

My father used to drink a lot
and get filled with rage, but sometimes he'd fall
into a strange combination
of melancholy and affection
for complete strangers, fellow drinkers
who were having hard times, too—
harder—and he had understanding.
I'd hear them stumble in the door,
my father likely singing verses
from a heartsick, gloomy song,
and then this stranger would be in the house.
The stranger had nowhere else to go
was the reason, then my father would hang
an arm over the stranger's shoulder,
his Good Samaritan routine.
It was kind of pitiful to be
a boy and have this going on.
My father would wake me up to meet
the stranger. And the stranger would humor me—
he'd pull a quarter from behind
my ear, or pop the false teeth
out of his mouth and suck them back,
like an animal who could do a trick.
One night, a giant appeared in our kitchen.
That's right, and his name was Mr. True.
He was over seven feet tall,
there wasn't any trick to that.
I thought he really was a giant,
he could hardly stand up straight in the room—
he didn't fit in a normal house.
In the morning I found Mr. True

still asleep on the floor. His feet
stuck out from the blanket, they looked
like a pair of fishing boats I'd seen
in books, absent the sails. Later,
he took me outside and set me high
upon his shoulders. It was higher
than I had ever been except
in a tree. I was a little sailor
perched at the top of a mast. And then
Mr. True teetered around
and dropped me on the shore of the porch,
and floated away forever. A lot
of my childhood was filled with sorrow,
as if someone had planted a garden of sadness
and lonely things were always blooming,
but once or twice it was magical.
I met a giant named Mr. True,
and I learned that taking in a stranger
is a decent thing to do, and you
can do it singing. Whatever torment
my father knew, he had a heart
for strangers and their suffering,
and a song to bring them through the door.

Minnesota
~ Gail Mazur

Here we are, a small gathering, and before us a figure at a podium
analyzing her dreams, a melodramatic exhibition of self-discovery …

Maybe because we're not psychoanalysts, her performance is less than
   riveting.

Yet though the others slip away I stay, as if I'm waiting for an insight
(that would surely prove—as so many insights have—useless, irrelevant.)

In the tiny low-ceilinged room, I'm now the entire audience.
My chair too small, tight, its arms binding my arms.

Was it one of the three bears that found one of the chairs too small?
The momma bear, trying the baby chair?

There are so many meanings, aren't there, of bear?

Child-sized, like the deco chairs on the Hindenburg.
The Hindenburg whose pink nose cone I passed daily in a filigreed yard.

Houston decades ago,

where I'd be out walking, the only pedestrian in Texas.
It could have been illegal.

The filigreed pink fence, and the filigreed reliquary
which held the cone also painted a pale pink …

The Hindenburg crashing and burning. From Germany.

The grand avenue in Houston shaded by live oaks, the silly frilly
    "nose cone."

But its nose would have been much too big for a lawn reliquary—

I suddenly realize that, an insight into my gullibility.
After all, I'd seen the movie.

Deco chairs—

Am I thinking of the burning deck the boy stood on when all but he
    had fled?
The chairs being re-arranged on the Titanic?

My house that burned in the night when I was seven?

My father, clinging to the breaking ladder?
The neighbors watching, titillated by nudity and calamity.

Heartless.

The speaker's fingers brush her tendrilly hair away from her cheekbones,
enacting a parodic drama of self-love, of trauma, of glamour

And now she no longer wants to walk alone in the woods—
too ugly, dark and deep.

No longer wants to recognize Indian pipe or monkshood.
To go barefoot on warm pine needles.

Will I never want that again either?
All the places we won't go, heedless, where are they exactly?

Looking for lady's-slippers in the hills of the Cotswolds?

Never to see Gloucestershire,
never to have scones with clotted cream among the English eccentrics?

The lady's-slipper, with its beautiful scrotum, the state flower of
    Minnesota.

I am very tired of the dreamer sharing her bad tidings.
Her browns, her siennas, her slithering snakes, her drowned palomino ...

This analysis could go several lifetimes while I sit in the burning dirigible,
my wrecking ball of a chair, my deco chair, listening.

Monkshood. Indian pipes. Lady's-slipper. Minnesota.

The significance of each figure may be clarified, fleetingly, questionably,
    in time.

But the significance of our dream—never.

dr27

Shade
~ Gail Mazur

—Alan Dugan, 1923–2003

A cold April day, five black ducks huddled,
shivering, on the bay, and coming to life, gardens
on Commercial Street we were all indifferent to.

Eight writers in a sort of circle arguing, ardent—
a committee living on argument, fierce, dismissive—
over eager youthful manuscripts, on fire

with the possibilities for poetry, as if we knew
the stakes, as if we could determine the future
of American literature in that bright sunny room.

Those meetings gripping, intoxicating, then—heaven—
all of us with passionate positions,
and adamant or uncertain, arguing the world.

And there sat our grumbly Dugan (but was he *ours*,
or anyone's?) in a chair apart, the least voluble among us,
hunkered down, muttering, decades past posturing,

if he'd ever postured, insistent, contrary—yet
the least excitable among us—as we all wrangled
for something we were sure was ours to shape.

Gone for good the Gauloises, gone for good the six-packs.
In his lap, page after page of illegible notations
on the yellow legal pad he'd scribbled on all winter

and kept to himself. Kept to himself, but he was *there*.
He'd told me once he'd always lost those battles—
I never actually saw him fight them, he'd read his notes

and sit, enclosed and silent, except to growl, deadpan,
Everyone's writing poems about Georgia O'Keefe. Or,
They all think they know Coltrane. Or,

Frieda Kahlo. Again. The implication:
no one but Dugan understood those three, and, dead,
they'd become drained, conventions, degraded

by callow enthusiasms. *I don't know if he's a poseur*,
he said once, *or if he just doesn't know what the hell
he's doing*. No exclamation points in Dugan, only judgments

thudding, resounding in the fierce room from the old poet
who in his distant Brooklyn boyhood was by his parents
nicknamed Spud—*Spud*: that boy impossible now

for us to imagine— *"How—I didn't know any word for it—
how 'unlikely'…"*

But today, more than a decade after his death, taking a stab
at sorting my papers, I find in a box some of Dugan's notes,
written on the back of a beat-up manila folder, lines

that stop me—that long-ago ephemeral Provincetown day
brought back tellingly in words I struggle to decipher
and transcribe, his handwriting illegible chicken—or rooster—

ballpoint scratches incongruously similar to Bishop's hand
on early drafts of "One Art":

Only 85—a long way to 100,
he writes, and

The darkness grew closer and darker
and he tried to see thru it to the other side,
fearless and undefeated
he died

On his deathbed—fought his sins to a draw
(I'm sure that's what this says.)
Then, a space, then one more word above a list I've written

of sandwiches for the committee's take-out lunch,
Shade
and in my tidy Palmer method, our choices:

2 lobster roll,
1 Greek salad,
4 fried sole sandwich
squid stew
3 lemonades,
coleslaw, fries, coke,
etc. etc.

Thinking of his bitter poems we so relish, I hear the same
unashamed intransigent voice in these oddly triumphant lines,
musical, destined for the wastebasket, scrawled when he was nearly 80,

half-lame, half-blind.... What makes me think, copying them here,
There is no music in hell—
Who believes in hell? Who believes in heaven?

The Monster Made of Bodies
~ Shane McCrae

What am I made of I am made of nobodies
and murderers
And thieves

and a whole family / The mother's
liver and her lungs
and the left half of the baby's face   / The doctor

Stitched it to the right half of the father's face
So that the smaller face
would pull the larger up

He said he thought
I would look happy but I see them
In the mirror every

Morning I have to even   I
In the morning have to   look I see them
staring at each other

not of   / Course with their eyes
but true and deep
Revulsion shapes the whole expression they

Stare with their foreheads and their mouths
Their noses and their cheeks / They stare
and each

struggles to push itself away from the other
Even when they are   calm they ripple at their edges
Like water just before it boils

None of this hurts
Not in the way you might expect
But still I can't get used to it

And in the gap that opens   if
you see me don't be frightened
It never opens very wide

I don't see blood I don't see   / The pulpy white
skin beneath skin or even
The skull itself half / A baby's skull and half a grown man's

but a different baby and a different man
I see green grass
A row of blades laid flat and close

My fingers are too fat
to fit inside the gap
But I have almost worked the courage up

To pry it open with the crowbar
The doctor   / Dropped when he fled
I think I would find earth beneath the grass

Anna Akhmatova (1903)
~ Campbell McGrath

Barely fifteen and already men are declaring
their love for her, grown men, and already she knows
she will drag their bodies across the white fire
of her nights as surely as she will sweep
the romance of the past behind her into this, her world.
She will bear the torch of the 19th century
into the present as Rilke carried a single iris
before his throat as he walked the streets of the city
to shield him from the monstrosity of mundane reality.

Ten years earlier, the first family photographs
are sepia prints: white gloves, a sailor's suit,
spring in the Crimea smelling of lilacs.
Ten years later, the first drawing is Modigliani's
erotic glyph, a sleek nude modernist arc,
the first paintings Cubist, Futurist, Acmeist.
Amid the studied decadence of the Stray Dog Café
she is a pale flower of the demimonde,
disdain for everything earthly and unexalted
scribbled in heroic stanzas across her face.
Ten more years and already she is famous
and already her voice is drowned
beneath the cadence of boots and rifles,
her verse denounced by Trotsky
as frivolously personal, archaically devout.
Another decade and she is reading Dante aloud
as Mandelstam weeps openly at the words—
mere words, mind you—days before the Party
swept him up in its grasp and he was gone.
She, who vowed to subsist on the sublime,
who could barely boil a potato or mend a sock,

living a life of denials and false confessions,
police officers knocking at the door,
the hasty burning of papers, again and again.
Why this portion for your children,
O Lord, terror and suffering and helplessness,
delivered from tyranny to tyranny,
day after day before the unblinking eye
of the prison gate, desperate for any word,
any sign of the vanished—why, O Lord?
Ten years to fame, twenty to famine,
thirty to the Terror, forty to the starving winter
of Leningrad under siege, fifty to the thaw,
sixty to an unanticipated old age
of vodka, ghosts and cabbage soup,
to the grey indeterminacy called,
in the corrupt modern idiom, life, real life.

Barely fifteen, smelling of lilacs and April rain,
already the men swearing passionate vows
not one of them intends to keep.

Edward L. Bernays (1928)
~ Campbell McGrath

People will buy anything if you make them want it bad enough,
if you give them something to chew on, a little skin,
a little rhubarb, an elbow in the ribs. Looking back, 1928
was the true birth of the Public Relations Industry,
when Lucky Strike cigarettes decided to sell smoking to women
and hired me to create the first professional P.R. campaign.
I never yet met a lady who wants to look fat, so the first act
was to promote cigarettes after dinner instead of dessert,
affidavits from medical bigwigs declaring cigarettes would save you
from the dangers of eating sweets, the Ziegfeld girls
testifying that Lucky Strikes kept them svelte, so by implication
not to smoke is to be a fat-ass tub of lard, a sow, a hag.
Still, smoking was "unladylike," so to crack that stigma
we came up with the Torches of Freedom march,
modern women parading down Fifth Avenue,
stylish, good-looking gals lighting up in public
as a protest against the oppression of their sex, the outrage
of being denied the right to kill themselves with cancer
on an equal footing with men, which is when I understood
that I could change anything, given time and money,
not just consumer choices but values, habits, social taboos.
The key is to leave no fingerprints, no paper trail,
to rely on indirect action through front organizations,
celebrity photo ops with matinee idols, expert testimony, lobbying
geared toward public fears aroused by one's own scare tactics.
People will buy anything if you hook them on the narrative—
bacon and eggs as health food, the liberation of Guatemala
on behalf of the United Fruit Company, beer as a bulwark
against intemperance. Last time I saw my Austrian uncle,
the famous Doctor Freud, we walked together in the Vienna woods
discussing family matters and the application of his theories,

not yet widely known in the USA—this was 1913 and I was
still a press agent working with show girls and vaudevillians,
coveting every column inch, pestering editors for ink,
so I understood the value of symbols and images, the power
of suggestion to shape desire, the need to ring the bells
that drive the herd—but how could I have known,
talking with Uncle Sigmund, how far his ideas would carry me,
that they'd find my book in Goebbels personal library after the war,
that the entire country would sell itself to the highest bidder,
that the President would end up packaged and marketed
like a box of frozen peas and carrots? Listen,
Henry Ford did not invent the car but who remembers
the name of the schmuck that did?
P.R. is my baby, no apologies, no regrets.
I wrote the rules and chopped the trees and paved the runway,
and when Felix Frankfurter denounced me to FDR
as a "professional poisoner of the public mind"
I admired a nimble piece of word craft, and I still consider it
as accurate a label as any my job will ever have,
but most of all I knew we had made it to the big time.
Greatest country in the world, America.
People will buy anything.

Obituary
~ Nancy Mitchell

Not stalled fog now, but smoke
rising from what are not lily

pads, but black holes
smoldering the water's

light-made lace, torched
by the river reeds. The farther

geese far flung
ash, the nearer, cinders.

It's newspaper split, a face
halved, no, not a heron

there folding into itself
on the dock.

Mon Père, Moi et Tout le Reste
~ Emmanuel Moses

On dirait mon père mais c'est moi
On dirait le soleil mais c'est la lune
On dirait un oiseau mais c'est un avion
On dirait le ciel mais c'est la mer
On dirait les étoiles mais ce sont des satellites
On dirait une forêt mais c'est un cimetière
On dirait une prière mais c'est une déclaration d'amour
On dirait une déclaration d'amour mais c'est une déclaration de guerre
On dirait sa fille mais c'est sa femme
On dirait sa femme mais c'est sa fille
On dirait un homme mais c'est une femme
On dirait de l'or mais c'est du fer
On dirait un feu d'artifice mais c'est un bombardement
On dirait des rires mais ce sont des pleurs
On dirait qu'il est vivant mais il est mort
On dirait qu'il est mort mais il est bien vivant
On dirait un paysage mais c'est un intérieur
On dirait un rêve mais c'est la réalité
On dirait un cauchemar mais c'est la réalité
On dirait un fou mais ce sont les autres qui sont fous
On dirait le soir mais c'est le plein midi
On dirait une flaque d'eau au loin mais c'est un mirage
On dirait une malédiction mais c'est une bénédiction
On dirait un souvenir mais c'est une prédiction
On dirait une répétition mais c'est la première fois
On dirait de la musique mais c'est une porte qui grince
On dirait un œil mais c'est un nuage
On dirait un nuage mais c'est un cygne
On dirait que c'est simple mais c'est compliqué
On dirait une larme mais c'est une perle
On dirait une épée mais c'est un rayon laser

On dirait une ville qui s'endort mais c'est une ville qui se réveille
On dirait un hôpital mais c'est un centre de détention
On dirait un secret mais c'est une annonce officielle
On dirait un bar mais c'est un temple
On dirait toi mais c'est ta sœur
On dirait moi mais c'est mon fils
On dirait l'espace mais c'est l'intérieur d'une boîte de conserve
On dirait du tissu mais c'est de la peau
On dirait l'au-delà mais c'est l'ici-bas
On dirait un démon mais c'est un ange
On dirait un enfant mais c'est un adulte
On dirait un arc-en-ciel tombé au sol mais c'est une tache d'essence
On dirait de l'encre mais c'est de l'eau
On dirait du vin mais c'est de l'encre
On dirait le courage mais c'est la peur
On dirait le commencement mais c'est la fin
On dirait la fin mais c'est le commencement

My Father, Me, and Everything Else
~ Emmanuel Moses, translated by Marilyn Hacker

You'd say it was my father but it's me
You'd say it was the sun but it's the moon
You'd say it was a bird but it's an airplane
You'd say it was the sky but it's the sea
You'd say those are stars but they're satellites
You'd say it was a forest but it's a cemetery
You'd say it was a prayer but it's a declaration of love
You'd say it was a declaration of love but it's a declaration of war
You'd say it was his daughter but it's his wife
You'd say it was his wife but it's his daughter
You'd say it was a man but it's a woman
You'd say it was gold but it's iron
You'd say it's fireworks but it's a bombardment
You'd say it was laughter but it's tears
You'd say he was alive but he's dead
You'd say he was dead but he's quite alive
You'd say it was a landscape but it's an interior
You'd say it was a dream but it's reality
You'd say it was a nightmare but it's real
You'd say he was a madman but it's the others who are mad
You'd say it was evening but it's high noon
You'd say it was a pool of water far off but it's a mirage
You'd say it was a curse but it's a blessing
You'd say it was a memory but it's a prediction
You'd say it was a repetition but it's the first time
You'd say it was music but it's a creaking door
You'd say it was an eye but it's a cloud
You'd say it was a cloud but it's a swan
You'd say it was simple but it's complicated
You'd say it was a tear but it's a pearl
You'd say it was a sword but it's a laser beam

You'd say it was a sleeping city but it's a city awakening
You'd say it was a hospital but it's a detention center
You'd say it was a secret but it's an official announcement
You'd say it was a bar but it's a temple
You'd say it was you but it's your sister
You'd say it was me but it's my son
You'd say it was space but it's the inside of a tin can
You'd say it was cloth but it's skin
You'd say it was the hereafter but it's the here-and-now
You'd say it was a demon but it's an angel
You'd say it was a child but it's an adult
You'd say it was a rainbow fallen to earth but it's a splotch of oil
You'd say it was ink but it's water
You'd say it was wine but it's ink
You'd say it was courage but it's fear
You'd say it was the beginning but it's the end
You'd say it was the end but it's the beginning

Marie
~ Carol Muske-Dukes

She moves through animal tragedy,
creatures crying out for pails of
mash she carries, one in each hand,

to a rippling trough—there for eager
feeding before death. Her dreams
teach themselves to undream now

Since death has taken her mother
& her own fortune. Framed certificate
& herself at a blackboard, scribbling

in lit chalk. *May 4, 1932.* Red sun
paves the way across parched fields,
bloodbright skies as she climbs a little

rise where Indian pipes, ghost-white,
light up. Her shoes begin to glow,
ruby in the sun's outstretching arm.

Her overalls filling with wind, her hair
standing, as the dust-devil lifts her,
spinning upward, pre-emptive, like her

once-stopless intent to write, write—
across lit clouds! O say her name, just
once: untied from the plowed earth, pails

rolling below. But no future can cry out
after her—Her little sister, my mother, runs
below, shielding her upturned gaze, calling "Marie!"

A name that she knows translates as: Stop flying!
Come down now to this heartless mothering
earth, this endless home, this hunger, Marie, Marie.

To Chief Leschi of the Nisqually
~ Duane Niatum

Long before Leschi was fitted with the hangman's knot,
he saw upon first meeting Isaac Stevens,
his nemesis who would someday sign his death warrant.
Stevens from his days as a young cadet
at West Point saw himself as Zeus
with a thunderbolt to strike the natives
from their land and wave in the white settlers
pouring into Nisqually Flats,
a swarm that flowed longer than the river.
With his sword always at the ready, Stevens
didn't need a flag because he carefully tattooed
on his large brow; *Manifest Destiny*,
as he strutted before
the Medicine Creek treaty officials
and the tribes that chose to attend.
With his very short legs, he cast himself
as an overlord of Olympian stature,
ignoring the fact he was barely five feet tall.
Choosing to see only the whites in his midst,
he reminded them what George Washington said
in 1793: that Indians and wolves were
both beasts of prey, though they have different shapes.
Bracing himself for the approaching hangman,
Leschi remembered it meant nothing to Stevens
that his ancestors had lived along the Nisqually
River for 10,000 years.
Stevens merely jeered, "So what."

After Reading Akhmatova
~ Duane Niatum

Sunset spoils the night at the heart;
I'm 77 years old and competing

with the old-growth cedar
for a little less weight down my spine.

I can read who is in the dark
or turn away at the outcome.

Symptoms
~ D. Nurkse

I traveled to the major cities, explaining my condition.

At first I only wanted to talk to the top specialist. Von Berg in Berlin, Porterhouse in Glasgow. Always as I spoke a trance came over me.

I could see myself from a distance of about ten feet, and hear my voice expounding, "my fibula itches, my femur seems displaced, I can't stop the hair inside my nose from growing,"—it was as if I could glimpse the world without me: the office, messy or immaculate, the doctor, with his expression of aggrieved boredom, perhaps a view of a dim street, where a nun might be walking a dachshund, or a child vanishing on a skateboard.

Know that when I cut myself shaving I bleed viridian. My urine is puce. I hear music constantly in my head. Themes that recur as rounds, then mirror fugues.

In Stockholm I found the expert who could understand why there was a hard bony shield fastened over my kneecap, but no, I had to explain it myself, while the surgeon took notes. As I positioned myself to see that script, he covered it with his hand. Lunging forwards, I saw the maze of cartoon faces.

Now I ride north, to find why the blood is spinning through my body, why my mind is filling with pictures that speak and take delight in each other, but don't know me and never shall: to Oulu, the white city of Kainu, Spitzbergen, Ultima Thule.

In the icebound clinics, frostbitten whalers huddle in corners, biting their lips. I find the old release, recounting a fresh development to a mining camp orderly, wrapped in scarves, or just to the Bic that hovers over the rexo'd form.

I tell the last famished sparrow how desire twists my body. It watches with bright oblique eyes and flies straight up.

Understand me: even the snow suffers, makes a wall against itself, and is transfixed by whirling lights.

Coyote After Field Fire
~ William Olsen

Of all the urban myths that feed on weakness,
the coyote has some meat to it, it bears itself, it takes it slow,
it takes it down whatever it is,
it is the gift
that jugulates the giver in its tracks
and eats until the myth is anorexic.

———————

Fucked-over animal is what it is.
It chews and swallows until its very thoughts are wholly
digested,
it walks forth on blackened feet, it crumpled to controlled burn
with not even grasshoppers grazing,
it looks as lost as glut,
it looks up to being looked at.

———————

Only after it begins to die—
who needs a myth for this—
does it lower its in-articulated, delectable eyes
and bare its teeth at earth.

———————

It is said to howl but it doesn't even sob,
not even after it throws off
flesh and bones does it sob,
not even after it is taken back by earth to a place of
further-than-ever incompletion

and its ribcage cradles the sooth and the pitiful poison,
of a wasp,
which lights on it, and pauses eternally....

Bare-Assed Hell
~ Dzvinia Orlowsky

Those who lied or mocked hanged on a hook from their tongues over a fire; those who forgot to fast hanged by their bellies ... Devils poured hot tar down Father's throat for drinking and for hitting Mother. Baba licked the hot frying pan because of her backbiting tongue and for being a great sorceress ...

—Alexander Dovzhenko, *The Enchanted Desna*

Punishment was punishment, not a game to be taken lightly, but when Mother condemned my sister and me to sit bare-assed on each other's bed pillows for *not sharing* the full-sized red velvet, satin-trimmed comforter while lying on the couch watching *Beat the Clock,* or for taunting each other with the tips of our peeled bananas, or for whining and kicking, because my foot crossed the line and touched hers, or hers, mine, we knew my family had arrived to another level of understanding: delivering an eye for an eye, or—as Mother preferred— *turning the other cheek.* My sister's or mine, it didn't matter.

She marched both of us into each other's rooms. Along the deep sky-blue carpeted hallway separating us from crime and punishment, we imagined dead ancestors greeting us, tongue-less and parched-throated, acknowledging us with sunken, sympathetic eyes, shrugging their shoulders as if to say *told you so.* My mother and sister spilled into my room first. My sanctum sanctorum. Had I been allowed to follow them, I would have bartered for amnesty with a few of my night table's most sacred relics: a fluorescent green wooly Willy Worm coiled to strike, the Avon Rapture Dusty Powder Puff, or my mini cactus with an artificial flower straight-pinned into its side. Mother went directly for my pillow, squeezing it like an accordion; then, thumping it between her fists, she tossed it against the wooden headboard. *Sit!* she commanded my sister. I could hear my sister whimper as she climbed onto my bed, gingerly lowering her behind on my cotton threads—*Shit*—! like a hen about to roost. In the next room, with my posture in check, I perched perfectly on my sister's feathered haven, taking in lingering sprays of Lemon and Heaven Scent Toilet Water. I was God's devout attendant, forward and gifted, potty trained in the art of remorse.

But, truth be told, I was a little concerned about the welfare of my behind. No matter how primly and properly we were raised, chances were good that we both sweated and drooled on our pillows during the night. On what, exactly, was I sitting? I had noticed that my sister's pillow had lost its fluff. It was lumpy and flat. It needed to see sunlight for a few hours. I was sure condemned souls and devils smoldered there.

But what if we shared *all things private* more than I dared to admit? We both crushed on Dick Semen and his younger brother, Mike. We both practiced (with high expectations regarding future crushes) giving hickeys on ourselves, covering the softest parts of our upper arms with light, blossoming bruises. We both loved pressing the down pillows against our faces, rubbing our lips back and forth against freshly washed cases, relishing the slight friction and welcoming heat, imprinting our budding desires and deep-seated secrets.

What if Mother, her kitchen timer set to 20 minutes, forgot about us—distracted by deadheading her roses? We had to stay put until she returned. I knew the drill: she would come to my sister first. *First girl, best girl* would quickly rise to a tear-filled apology. Reluctant at first, Mother would withhold for a few seconds before finally releasing her from guilt, her fanny all damp from lack of ventilation. I imagined her pressing down a little extra hard against the sheets as she slid off my bed.

Now free, she wanted me still seated, exposed and vulnerable. We had become fixed features in each other's dreams. What was hers was now mine. What was mine had become hers. Squatting rights. To her, I was nothing more than an ass—wider and heavier than a storm cloud—more pathetic than our ancestors who slurped cream or fried eggs with ham during fasts, who were forced to sit, throughout eternity, bare-bottomed on hot frying pans...

Dick, meet my sister...

Q&A: Insurance
~ Alicia Ostriker

If time is an arrow, what is its target

If a Flexible Flyer is the sled I had as a child, when may I become a
    child again

Do you need help to dig the potatoes of insults out of your garden

Do you plan to vote in the next election

Is our country headed in the right direction or the wrong direction
    and what did the jackhammer tell the yellow helmet's ear

Which part of your body is like biting into a ripe peach
    which part shames you like a rotten peach

Would you like to find out how to lower your interest rate

When you go to heaven how old will you choose to be
    will you have cocktails on the well-watered lawn
        where Bach conducts Bach

Will you still chase after the Grateful Dead

Is your life like air leaking out of a balloon, or like rain falling on a pond
    dot dot dot   dear pocks   pocking the surface   dot dot dot

Can it be like snow falling on the ocean

Can desire drown you like syrup over pancakes

When an ambulance siren wakes you at 3 a.m. do you feel relieved
                not to be strapped to that stretcher
      speeding toward the grim unknown
      do you then snuggle next to someone

Are you satisfied with your detergent

Can you name a more perfect irony than the new world trade center,
      symbol of capitalism, lingam of profit, soaring above the pools
           dedicated to the memory
                  of people killed when the first towers fell

Can you describe the scent of dried blood

What about the smell of iron chains in your cell
Can you sing the threnody of the maggots

When I removed my mask did I frighten you
      like a drone crossing your sky   *

Are you satisfied with your auto insurance

When ecstasy approaches why do you resist
    What are you afraid of
        Can you please unbutton your shirt now

The Light
~ Alicia Ostriker

What is the birthplace of the light that stabs me with joy
and what is the difference between avocados sold on the street
by a young man conceived in Delhi and avocados sold

by cornrow girls in the West Side Market, I am anyhow afloat
in tides of Puertorican, Cuban, Mexican, Westindian Spanish, wavelets
     of Urdu
rolling like oceans, sweating like jackhammers, rasping like crows,
     calling out

in the West Side Market, the Rite Aid and every other shop on the street
Porque no comprendes, you don't own this city any more
the city belongs and has always belonged to its shoals of immigrants

crashing ashore in foaming salty droplets, *como no, gringita—*
with their dances and their grandmothers, with their drinking and
     their violence
and their burning yearning to be free, and smelling money, what, what
     is the joy

is it those lamps of light those babies in their strollers
those avocados with their dark-green pebbled rinds, shining from inside
two for four dollars in the West Side Market, and three for four dollars
     from the cart

joy like white light between the dollar bills, is it these volleys of light
     fired
by ancestors who remember the projects, the sweatshops, the war,
who supposed their children's children would be rich and free?

Where a Few Things Come From
~ Ruth Padel

Tidings (noun):

'News, intelligence, announcement. Message received and
understood. Good news.'
First used in the twelfth century. From Middle English *tiding*,
tithand, 'report,
a piece of news', Old Norse *tīdhendi*, 'events' and *tīdhr* (adj.)
'occurring.'
'Update'—as in *Tidings of great joy, which shall be to all the people.*

Tide (noun):

Old English *tid*, 'due time, a point or slice of time. A period, a
season,'
from Proto-Germanic **tidiz*, 'division of time', PIE **di-ti-*
'division,'

and suffixed form of **da* meaning 'cut up.' Cognate with Sanskrit
dati, 'cuts', Greek *demos*, 'people, land' and *daiesthai*, 'divide.'

(*Divide? Why all this division?*) Also 'rise and fall of sea,'
late Middle English, fourteenth century, from notion of fixed time

so 'time of high water', possibly from Middle Low
German *getide*, Dutch *tij*, 'flood tide, a swell of sea.'

Old English had no word for this. *Flod* and *ebba* were 'rise' and
'fall.'
And *Heahtid*, 'high tide', meant 'high day, festival.'

Tide (verb):

          'To happen" (Old English),
                'carry, as the tide does' (1620s)
                      usually with 'over'

Shelter (verb):

        'To screen
            protect
                take shelter' (1580s)

Shelter (noun):

'Structure affording protection' (1580s). possibly
from Middle English *sheldtrume*, 'roof or wall
formed by locked shields.' From 1890
onward, 'temporary lodging for the homeless poor.'

Empathy, Sympathy, Compassion (nouns):

From *en-* and *sun-pathein* (Greek),
pateor and *cum* (Latin),
'feeling with' or 'feeling in.'

Ability to identify with distress.
Neural response of a divided brain
hard-wired to feel another's pain.

From The Hospital Waiting Room
~ Linda Pastan

Your mother,
at a hundred and four, clings
to her life as to a raft
that might still save her,
even as it drifts out to sea.
She's misplaced
her doctor's name,
misplaced the name of the season
performing in full view
outside her window—
how can so much snow
spill from the sky?
Surely the pitcher
will be emptied soon.
And though she says
she's lived too long already,
at the slightest dizziness—
that cruel cerebral static—
she calls for help.
In the waiting room
we wait. Has the clock
simply lost its mind?
Is life too cheap or too dear,
and how on earth to spend it?

The Heaven of Lost Earrings
~ Molly Peacock

Go down the grate after the green
agate scarab with the frowny face,
then through the damp and the dark
—the heaven of lost earrings is not
a bright place. Curl with the crumbs
in the corner of a pocket in
the discarded clothing bin,
then climb up the unzipped flap
of a suitcase and meet me
next to the severed pearl.
In the velvet dark of reattachment,
through beach sand and grime
in lintballs, dustballs, dirtballs soft
as the earlobes they were lost from,
next to the carved blue lapis orb—

through the crack in the floor, beneath
the taxi seat, in the accordion seam
of a subway train, in the airplane toilet
on another plane altogether where a low
moan replaces the harp and keens,
"There must be two, there must be two,"
hurtling toward the midnight of reunions
where everyone forgets what started
their arguments, why one unclasped
so suddenly, or the other's stud just
dropped without a sound to bury itself
in a carpet in a lobby and the loop
that contained the red droplet
with its cloisonné leaf sprang
down the cleft in an elevator shaft

after it, almost like Orpheus calling for
Eurydice, meet me.

              The heaven
of lost earrings is not a hell, though
it's dark *down* there that becomes *up* here
on the other side of the world where
memories surface, carrying their own light
unlike the heaven of the airy risen.
This is a heaven of the fallen
where each fleck, each gold whorl,
each silver hinge gleams up in the murk
for its partner, searching through the rubble,
sniffing for the button-y smell of the other
till they click and clasp their clasps
or slide long wires into their studs at last
and glow not as on a stage or even in the light
of a windowsill, but as in the warmth
of an unmade bed just left by the gods
up hungry for their nectar, now
nestling alone, forgotten but for a stab
in the nerve-end lightning of a memory flash:
meet me down there in the fold.

What the Lost Are For
~ Carl Phillips

Here, before these shadows that,
in their disappearing, returning,
then falling as softly again
elsewhere, have sometimes
seemed the first and last lesson
left on the nature of power, though
they are not that, I bow my head,

I bend my knee. I hardly care,
I think, anymore who goes there,
only let me pass—however
flawed—among them, my fears
not stripped from me, but kept
hidden as, more often than not,
just beneath stamina, somewhere

grace, too, lies hidden. Nobody
speaks to me as you do. Nowhere
water-lit do the leaves pale faster.

La Montagne Fermée
~ Gabriel et Marcel Piqueray

Que cela traîne !... Fameux travail, pourtant, si haut, interminable.
L'Homme invisible.
Une fusée éclairante part et siffle, sans plus ; lentement retombe,
    éteinte, à côté de quatre moutons morts.
Une femme, cheveux à l'odeur de pain frais et d'eau tiède, quarante
    ans, géologue, se penche vers une roche.
Entre ses lèvres, on perçoit un mot qui évoque l'amour. Encore un
    mort.

The Sealed Mountain
~ Gabriel and Marcel Piqueray, translated by Robert
  Archambeau and Jean-Luc Garneau

How slow it is! Glorious, endless work, no matter how high you climb.
The invisible Man.
A flare goes off whistling, falls back slowly, and snuffs out next to four
    dead sheep.
A woman, smelling of fresh bread and of warm water, forty years old,
    a geologist, stoops, examining a stone.
You can just make out the love-words on her lips. Another corpse.

L'Amoureux
~ Gabriel Piqueray

pour Yih-Ching, à Luc Rémy, to Dexter Gordon

Sa longue expérience de la solitude le rend attentif aux ébats des
 mouettes.
Pour le moindre biscuit, le plus petit quignon de pain lancés ver elles,
 éclatent leurs disputes criardes.
Mais elles sont, toujours, ensemble.
Arrivé à ce point de ses références, cet observateur curieux porte un
 regard émerveillé aux premières vagues de l'Océan, s'assied sur le
 banc et se met à rêver.
Bientôt les promeneurs, qui s'approchent de l'Amoureux, doivent,
 très vite, se rendre à l'évidence.

(dernier poème, Septembre 1991)

The Lover
~ Gabriel Piqueray, translated by Robert Archambeau
and Jean-Luc Garneau

for Yih-Ching, to Luc Rémy, to Dexter Gordon

His long solitude sharpens his attention to the frolic of seagulls.
They fight noisily for the smallest crumbs and the tiniest crusts of
    bread.
Yet they remain, always, together.
Far past his last point of reference, a bystander, he gapes in awe at the
    roiling waves of the virgin sea, settles himself on a park bench,
    begins to dream.
Soon the strolling passers-by, finding the lover, will feel the cold shock
    of the truth.

(last poem, September 1991)

House Sitter
~ Kevin Prufer

After her fifth drink she felt light-headed
and hadn't the strength to climb out of the hot tub.

So good
            just to rest there,
leaning back in the water.

And then she couldn't open her eyes—they'd grown
hot, her whole body emptied,
                              soothed and glowing,

and lovely
            to listen to the water churn,
the gentle pulse that emptied her of words,

until a feeling, like static, overwhelmed her
and she slipped
                underwater.

+

The little yellow jewel in the bottom of her glass said,
That was easy.

The ounce of liquor that sweetened the bottle:
Too, too easy—

And the drowned woman in the hot tub shifted in its currents,
staring at the starry sky—

+

For a few nights, raindrops disturbed the water's surface.
So much rain that season,
                              then dying leaves
thickening the lens she looked through.

A wind had toppled the wine glass
                              that lived now in its surprising
shards. *Nothing to it,*
                    the bottle replied
from the hot tub's edge.

+

The water turned her over in its mind
like an idea,
                    easily grasped at first,
but later filled with complexities it hadn't considered:
What had powered her laughter
                              and where did it go?
Her cell phone long ago stopped ringing.
Had it nothing left to tell her?
                         At what point
was she no longer herself?
                         At what point
did she become merely
the hot tub's contents?

+

She is a useful metaphor for me
when I think of people I have loved
who now are gone.
                    Memories of the dead

fill us as a body fills a tub. In the process, they displace
other thoughts and memories.

For instance:
listening to rain tap on the windows
or surprised by the first scent of fall,

I want my father back.
And so experience my father's absence
as a displacement
                        of volume.

+

Nothing to it, the bottle said,
half-filled with murky rainwater—

+

So the dead woman grows blue
and foreign as the leaves
                        cover her up. She changes
shape within the mind that holds her, she leaks.

What part is her
and what part is water?

I wish I could believe we are held within the minds of others
and never vanish.

+

And what about the owner of the house?
He had enjoyed a lovely time away
and now, after a month,
                                    returned to find
the hot tub churning and uncovered.

And when he swept the leaf rot from the water's surface
and looked down into the brown
                                    depth,
he felt only horror.
                        A leg, atilt. Fingers split.
A swirl of half-concealing hair:
The water holding her in its thoughts.

+

I'm still talking about my father.
I think I've exposed myself too much here.

After the Fall of the House of Usher
~ Lawrence Raab

Sometimes I think I made it all up,
that if I returned I'd be told
there'd never been a house beside that tarn—
who would build anything in such a place?

But I'm not asking you to believe
a story you probably never thought was true,
at least in the way we used to think
about the truth, meaning that it happened.
I'm just looking back, since I can see

my own death not so far away, and I worry
that what I wrote feels too *excited*,
too eager to create *effects*, though I like effects.
Beauty and terror—how companionable
they were in those days! But at the end

I really was afraid. I know you want
to hear why we put her in the tomb,
then screwed the lid of the coffin down.
Couldn't we have left the poor woman
alone in her bed, let her wake up,
if she was going to, as if from a dream?

What can I say?—it didn't occur to me
at the time. I'm not a doctor, just a friend
and a narrator. She had physicians, I specifically
mention that fact, and I saw her
only once, briefly, far across the room.

Of course Usher knew. He could hear her
rustling around in the dark, figuring out
where she was. And then he called *me* mad—
"*Madman, I tell you that now she stands
without the door!*" That's close enough

to what he actually said, and I remember
feeling unnerved and taken aback.
Why was he yelling *at me?* Then the wind
tore everything apart, and we saw her.

Yes, I've changed a few of the details
but it's been so long I couldn't say which ones.
I must have thought that another touch
of atmosphere might help convey
the way it was. Yet how ordinary
so many strange things turn out to be,

like dreams that end up disappointing us
by making sense. Look,
I wasn't there to save anyone.
I just tried to be his friend.

Morir Sonando
~ Martha Rhodes

He looks over at her body, at rest,
examines the Tuscan peach plaster walls he built,
the six generous windows of their bedroom,
its black granite floor, massive oak armoire,
and looks away, toward the French doors,
marble balcony, freshly seeded lawn,
to the sandy path, and finally the beach itself
where the wash of waves against his thighs
turns him blue, even as he dresses in his closet,
for he has left her already; he is lost at sea.

The Artist Travels Incognito
~ Susan Rich

after Leonora Carrington

She loved to cook surreal meals with medieval recipes,
the ingredients, by necessity, improvised.

Sometimes in the middle of the night she clipped
hair from her guests' redheads

and then served their contributions in the next day's buttery soup.
Culinary experimentation, the artist called it,

and carried on spreading homemade mustard along the edges
of her heels and then, toes, whenever conversation bored her.

In her painting *Grandmother Moorhead's Aromatic Kitchen*,
mischievous women bake miniature pies in a wine-colored salon.

Apparently, they're good friends who, cloaked in monastic robes,
share a resemblance with prehistoric birds. And perhaps it's the
     playfulness

of their sun-glassed masks or the friendly goose in bluestockings,
slightly right from the picture's center, but the festive atmosphere

is not unlike the afternoon hours we covet in the House of Sky.
Instead of homemade pies, you bring dark chocolate dipped

in rosewater and I offer Mexican almonds, pomegranates and tea.
Together we pick lines, sing them back and forth from favorite books

or we fill a box with paper scraps, hand-printed with directions for
    invention.
Write a story with a bird in it, unusual soup, an unanswerable
    question—

the paper states and we set the kitchen timer, begin to work—
our images half-baked, half-other worldly.

And perhaps this friendship *is* a type of madness, this seeking
of the luminous in a fine line of words; the lyric as rose-colored
    chalice—

but how better to spend our lives than in rooms of imagination and
    surprise?
Like the bird women in the kitchen, we gild our alchemical lives.

for Kelli Agodon

Salaryman
~ David Rivard

In the plume of smoke rising
from a volcano on the coast of Iceland,
papery sheets of ash—each ripped square
like a note safety-pinned
to a child's woolen coat
but torn off by a roadside wind—

a missing explanation—

"Please help this boy," the note reads,
"he is a good boy. Give him only
what is needed. He will be
neither genius nor dolt. He likes thinking
(as if thinking were the same
as swimming). When he hears
the hum of bees in the honey locust
teach him that a barge song
is what the bees sing. Remind him
that the lake is there for him to swim—
he doesn't always need to think. This
is a world where a shy salaryman
with a handful of supermarket roses
wrapped in cellophane has to walk
under a sky full of falling rain—
tell this boy the threadbare & blushing
could use a spokesman too."

I Apologize in Advance
~ Ira Sadoff

but nothing delights me more than eating pussy.
More than imaginary strolls with Picasso
or the yellow sea that swirls in that hot Panang curry.

If you've lived in the world, you know there's little wisdom
to dispense: you duck arrows from whichever empire
scribbles down your thoughts the minute that you dream them.

In the end maybe you get one idea to keep to yourself,
but who's to say it's yours? Our minds are little magnets.
bad radios with competing voices from Cincinnati

and Chicago. As for eating pussy, it takes complete trust
in the tongue, complete concentration, opening up
for someone you love: those unfathomable moans give way

to whines and whispers before slipping into sighs
and melody. I mean the whole body becomes a dancer's
body: sinewy, lithe, satin. And once you've stripped down

the niceties and icicles that make us models of decorum,
you can open the window and your neighbors' voices
will seem startlingly human. Trivial and impossible.

Advantage Federer
~ Mary Jo Salter

The Holy Roman Empire comes to mind
tonight, as I sit among the nineteen thousand
in Madison Square Garden, which is not
anywhere near Madison, nor is it square,
nor is it a garden.

Still, even Voltaire
could have found something holy about it,
partly because the real Placido Domingo
is in the stands, enduring the microphone
somebody jams in his face on the Jumbotron;

and also because, loud as opera, in a cloud
of dry ice from the locker room pit,
a herald's voice proclaims that it is Fed
himself parting the crowd, and by god that's him,
the Greatest of All Time.

His opponent gets some hoopla, but how can he rate?
I scrutinize Roger's legs (shapely and human,
in shorts trimmed by a gold tuxedo stripe)
with the same imploring attention I've seen him train
on the face of his racket

in close-ups on TV; and look, he's doing it now,
plucking pensively at the Wilson logo,
the W in the mirror: *I am the man,
I can do this.* All the chanters agree he can:
let's go, Roger, let's go!

And yet… although our tickets buy us space,
time is an ace; the match is whizzing by.
First set, second, third. Now he has lost.
Now all the talking, graying heads can say
into their cameras gravely: how long can he last?

Oh, but elation has the highest ranking!
Surely I'm winning, simply by being alive
while Roger Federer is thirty-three
and playing like an angel and gamely thanking
the sponsors and the up-and-coming Dimitrov:

"I'd like to thank Grigor for beating me."
Seventh Avenue is seventh heaven
as I float out into the evening, hardly aware
of the rain when I open my umbrella's face
to stare into it, as Federer might stare.

Image Worship
~ Grace Schulman

Faces on the lid of the Knabe Grand
caught my eyes when I tried *The Happy Farmer*,

dreaming of ploughs far from my rutted sidewalks.
Digging, not earth but notes, and neither happy

nor a farmer, I hit wrong keys,
taunted by the metronome. As a distraction,

I stared at smiles in silver frames. War dead.
I never knew them. Heavy-fingered, longing

for their lightness, I saw an uncle waving;
somebody's hell-raiser climbing an oak;

an aunt, a doctor, silk scarf blown in wind.
Suddenly my face appeared among the faces

soon to hide or be interred. The woman's
deep-set eyes in the black-white photograph,

mine in the frame glass, merged, until
the wind lifting her scarf blew through me.

Now, when I stir to brighter images—
a yellow coat, a fawn's sleek arabesque—

I think of photographs, and of Aeneas,
who, in a strange city, stunned by a shrine

with pictures of his own city's destruction,
a burning palace, the dead, cried out:

sunt lacrimae rerum: there are tears in things.

Née-Décédé
~ Martha Serpas

We were seated around the Thanksgiving table—
turkey, stuffing, potatoes *au gratin*—
eight or ten of us, when I noticed,
as I passed on the green beans and slivered
almonds, that they were all dead:

gelatin-eyed, orifice-oozing, putrefying dead.
I hadn't detected the strong smell above the broccoli
casserole and crusty Brown 'n Serve rolls.

I had been passing the wine, passing the water,
talking to myself about my affairs.

As their fingers lifted slightly from the table,
I laid coins on their eyes and kissed their brows.
I freed the dogs, who seemed warm, from their filthy pens.

One shouldn't look for the living among the dead.

Back at the farm where my father, dishes done,
moves a stick through ryegrass,
and a sharp-tailed snake heads for a thicket.
He wanders below Douglas firs and
smokes a Kool cigarette.

In the mornings I lie with him in the orchard and watch
the elk calves leap like static.
Sometimes a young bull. Mostly
cows clowning, distracting us while their cow
friends unlace liberty apples
                from the lowest branches.

He hasn't aged. His nose is still broken
and his knuckles are a size too large.
For July his skin is burned patriot red,
and his eyes are green, green, green.

The hyphen between his dates is so tiny, carved
into the mausoleum's marble, it is a freckle,
half an ellipsis.
It's meant to pull the years one
on top the other. It's meant to erase
itself, like an iris wipe before The End.

On the farm I cut the grass with a push mower.
I try to save the wren's nest I dislodged
with the cane knife—his—
that I had been swinging through the brambles.
I nail new shingles on the porch steps when it rains.

Every morning I bring you tea in bed is his tomorrow.
The tray empty, the kettle and steam quiet,
the bricks fire-polished and weightless as they fall.

Stele
~ Alan Shapiro

3rd century BCE Greek

The mother's face in profile—
looking toward foreign sunlight
pouring in through the window—
is looking from the upper fragment,
which is rounded at the top
and crumbled inward
toward the bottom
where her neck and shoulder
ought to be, where only wall is now.
The bottom of it balances,
or seems to, on the fragment under it
of a robed breast, under which
on the mother's lap the arm
descending from the missing
shoulder surrounds a baby
squirming to look up and back
at something over the shoulder
that isn't there.
The mother's face
is stately, composed, almost absurd
in its dignified stiff refusal
to acknowledge that her robe's
been pulled back and bunched
up high on her thigh
by all the baby's squirming
to see whatever it is
behind the mother
that in the stopped
instant of the scene

somebody else, the husband
maybe, had wanted put there
to remind himself
until he joined them in the tomb
of just how curious
in life the baby was,
how patient the mother.

It is as if the mother thinks
that time has stopped for the two of them,
or would stop if only
the foreign sunlight
wasn't inching every moment
closer to illuminate
a restlessness and patience
long since out of date.
If only it wasn't seeping
up her thigh now, over
the bunched robe and squirming baby,
brightening on the wall
a moment where the neck and shoulder
should have been before
it rises to the face,
which almost seems to
harden against its own
illumination, so as to preserve
the pretense that it isn't
centuries away and doesn't
know she's just a figure
on a tomb that's crumbled out
from under her to these
broken pieces of a raft
they drift apart on without moving,

she and the baby, lost
as the sunlight of a day
two thousand years ago
this sunlight imitates,
pouring in and washing
over and carrying away
with subatomic patience
both the patient mother
and the restless child who
in her very stillness
won't sit still, twisting
and squirming to
glimpse behind the mother
whatever it was in life
she couldn't wait to see.

Keats
~ Alan Shapiro

I saw my brother David last night across the gym head bent in conversation with someone I couldn't see very well. As I approached David didn't look up to acknowledge me or break off the conversation or introduce me to his friend. It was as if I wasn't there, as if I were the one now who is supposed to do the haunting. As his companion said something I couldn't catch in a voice I almost recognized, David smiled and looked up in my direction; it was a knowing smile, but what the smile knew it wouldn't tell me. The smile was the withholding of what it seemed to say and thus was how it said, "You can't know anything about it, not even what it is." Then he stepped aside, and there I was, as I had once been, forty years ago. Twenty-three years old, and I was holding a book of Keats's letters, opened to a letter Keats, when he was twenty three, had written to his brother, and in the letter this was italicized: "Our bodies every seven years are completely fresh-materiald.... Tis an uneasy thought that in seven years the same hands cannot greet each other again." The book was floating in the hands of who I was when I still had brother, and the words meant nothing to me, just dead marks on a page. I could see right through the ghost of me, a chalky shadow of a hand holding the book out for me to read while the hand said, "This hand can't greet that hand." Then the band I hadn't noticed launched into a silent number, and people filled the dance floor, and the boy stepped into my brother and disappeared, both lost now to the man I was there among the silent dancers as that man will be to the old man I'm becoming. A fresh-materiald ghost in waiting suddenly dis-haunted by the ghost I was, a ghost made even more remote and insubstantial, by the words of an even deader boy whose voice out of the book I now was holding was speaking such immediate unease he seemed just then more alive than I or my brother ever was, or anyone living.

My Father
~ Alan Shapiro

To him, business was all that mattered. And in business you either gave a fucking or took a fucking. Unfortunately, he was almost always the one who took, not the one who gave, whereas according to him I was a chemist when it came to money: if I had it I turned it into shit. The few times he had it he invested in the stock market, and the investments mostly tanked or flatlined, until he sold them, then they rose. Still ever hopeful he'd explain: "You have to speculate to accumulate. The only thing that grows when you hold it is your pecker." Of a man who had no taste in clothes he'd say his collar didn't match his cuff. Of a man he didn't trust, he'd say, "He'd fuck a snake if he could get down low enough." When I was twelve, and it was time, according to my mother, for me to know about "the birds and bees," he called me into the bedroom while he was cleaning his golf shoes with a knife, digging dried mud out from between the cleats and flicking the bits and pieces onto the newspaper at his feet. Head bent over the upturned shoes, he never looked up or paused in his work. "Al," he said, "you're almost a man now, so keep it covered. Now get lost." When I told him I wanted to be a poet, he asked me if I was queer? One Sunday afternoon, my brother and I were roughhousing with him on the floor of the den, which we often did and loved doing though it was frightening, which was part of the fun, how truly manic he would get, eyes crazed, mouth frothing, speaking some foreign tongue made of grunts and laughter as he threw us up and down against each other, tickling us just hard enough for us to feel what else he could do if he decided to, communicating through the play a violence way beyond the play, and from someone where else in the house my mother came running, thinking we were screaming in earnest, which we may have been: "Get off them," she cried, "get off them!" and raised her hand as if to strike him and he scrambled up from the floor so quickly she fell back against a wall and now his hand was raised and she was cowering, arms up like a shield in front of her face—quietly he said, "Don't ever," and the menace in the quiet said playtime was over. If he saw a white woman with a black man in public walking arm in arm, he'd say under his breath, "Take him home to meet your mother." Then to us he'd say, "When you walk through a field of clover you smell like clover; when you walk through a field of shit you smell like shit." Yet on her deathbed he begged his own daughter, whom he'd disowned for marrying a black man, to forgive him for his stupid bigotry. What he never thought of didn't exist until he thought of it, which he seldom did. My mother called him the most selfish man she'd ever known. He called her a frigid bitch. If anything was wrong with any of us, he'd be sick with worry but otherwise he didn't need to see us, often didn't want to see us, and when he did see us couldn't wait for us to leave. Once he retired and until he went blind, he watched CNBC all day long, following the stock prices passing in the crawl bar at the bottom of the screen. We had almost nothing to say to each other. He was short-tempered, bullheaded, anxious, unreflective, handsome, loyal, charming, utterly miserable in his marriage but otherwise, as he would put it, "A-okay, copacetic, aces."

Superman Attempts Rescue of Philosophical Dilemma, Fails
~ Jeffrey Skinner

Be honest—if what we call *nothing* actually existed
who would be the one to report it? Consciousness added
to nothing is no longer nothing. It's one, added to zero.
And if you think death plunges us into nothing
that thought also requires the I, which you call lost
in death. Ok: maybe self rises from, is adjunct to, matter,
disappearing with the body. But we can't locate the I
in the body, nor do we understand how it might arise
from any congress of cells. We can only sense
some cloudy version of nothing when mind is present,
never one apart from the other. Which turns everything
on its head! As if Clark Kent could only have being
when seen at the same time as Superman, & Superman
only exist *with* Clark. And this, of course, is the truth—
as we the viewer, the observer, the comic-book page turner,
the mind without a home, have always known.

Full-Size Rendering
~ Jeffrey Skinner

Here is a sentence with the same features as the one it loves.
The just read sentence has gone spinning into space, while the other
remains on the page. They are entangled: whatever happens
to one happens to both, no matter how far apart.
Once you've read one you've read the other
and neither can be unread nor lost. The sentences watch
each other through a knothole in time;
time has a grain you can cut against, or with.
It is where you and your beloved speak, briefly, of city life.
When the map is unfolded and laid flat on the wooden table,
ridges smoothed down with a gigantic palm, *then*: you feel that gaze,
you know there is no place for death to hide these words.

Spoiled
~ Tara Skurtu

You don't know how to give
your words to the world this morning,
so you get out of bed, grab a shirt
from the pile of worn shirts, take
a walk to the corner market. I'm listening
to the man in the apartment below sing
ooh don't you wanna take her home,
and you're half asleep picking through
a bin of fruit. You come back to bed
with a perfect apple, put it in my palm.
So small, so red. I can't wait to eat it
alone. I shut the door behind me
in the kitchen and turn on the news.
Two dumbfounded men lean over
the world's new largest loaf
of rustic potato bread, 96.6 kg.
The man below the apartment sings
ooh don't you wanna break her.
I bite the apple and wish
I hadn't—the flesh mealy, a mouthful
of sweet mashed potatoes I spit
into the garbage. The news anchor eyes
the big mound of bread like a trampoline,
the other man pierces it with a serrated knife.
A perfect yeasty line of steam mists
up and out of the screen, warming
this room where I sit holding the world's
most horrible apple, listening to Romanian
Blondie on a loop, and to you, in the shower
down the hall, scrubbing the sweat
of our morning from your skin.

Une accusation dans la rue
~ Ron Slate

Owing to an incautious aspect of my nature which has often delayed my arrivals and sometimes led to crises, I walked straight toward the shouting and passed by the market on the Rue de Seine, a shopping list in my hand.

The two were arguing on the sidewalk, the woman striding away, then stopping to turn back and abuse the man who in turn would halt a few steps behind her. I understood quickly that she had bought some tulips in the flower shop and he, a clerk there, had followed her out of the store where some part of the transaction had gone awry.

Yes, she had ordered some irises as well, but he had sold the last of the white ones she preferred.

The desire to please—suppose there is a child who can do nothing to assuage the fear and despondency of the mother. Trying to gratify her diminishes, hour by hour, the chance for something. What is it?

Now the space between the woman and man was growing, her paces were of a uniform length but his steps were losing intention. Under the repeated punishments of her remarks, he became calmer. He looked up at the sky or maybe at a high window.

Scribbled on the other side of my list—walking to the market, overcoming all resemblances within the very pith of resemblance, neither to search the streets and help complete her arrangement nor to buy some flowers in the man's shop to restore his benign routine of commerce. Mid-day hour of acts undone.

Radishes, shallots, lemons, lettuce.

Cruising for Poetry
~ Tom Sleigh

after Carlos Drummond De Andrade

If poetry comes up to you to stare you down,
you'll freeze like the winter sun
unmoving in the sky, neither bright or warm.
So don't write poetry about what people tell you
are life's greatest events.
Nothing gets born, nothing dies in poems.

Forget your affinities, birthdays, your life's little occasions—
none of that counts. And don't write poetry
with your body, that too complete, comfortable,
self-sufficient body so hostile
to the poem overflowing its bright banks.
Your drop of bile, your smile or frown
of pleasure or grief in someone's darkened room—who gives a shit?
So don't blather on and on about your feelings—
all they'll do is mislead you with ambiguous understandings,
they'll con you and take you for a ride.
And whatever your brain, distracted, tells itself it thinks,
forget it—that's still not poetry.

Don't celebrate the city, leave all that concrete in peace.
Song shrugs off the cars moving in the streets,
it turns its back on the paltry secrets inside houses.
No matter what you think, it's not music overheard
flowing down from an open window,
and it sure as hell isn't the surf beating its forehead on the sand.
Song isn't natural or anything to do with nature,
and as for people getting along and calling themselves citizens,
song doesn't give a damn.

For it, rain and darkness, exhaustion and hope,
don't mean a thing. And don't think that poetry
wants anything to do with objects
though it's been known to make subjects and objects one.

Don't go in for melodrama, don't conduct mystical investigations,
above all, don't invoke some idiot god.
Don't waste time lying. Don't give in to exasperation.
Your yacht of ivory, your diamond-studded shoes,
your peasant dances and superstitions, your family skeletons
will only disappear into the way time curves,
they're worse than useless.

Don't shove at us your buried and oh-so-pathetic childhood.
Don't confuse what you've seen in the mirror
with what you think you can recall.
Look, if it's faded, it wasn't poetry.
And if it broke, it wasn't crystal.

Enter as quietly as you can into the realm of words.
That's where poems are waiting to be written.
They may lie there paralyzed, but they aren't in despair,
they're refreshed in the calm of unbroken surfaces.
Look at them, isolate and silent, pure beings of the dictionary.

Live inside your poems before you write them.
Don't get annoyed if they're obscure.
If they poke and prod you, don't lose your cool.
In the silence inside words, each word
waits to show itself before it disappears.

Don't force the poem to tear itself from limbo.
Don't go picking up lost poems off the floor.

Don't flatter the poem with high-flown bullshit.
Accept it in the same way that it will have to accept its form
defining and concentrating the space around it.

Get down on all fours and take a good look at the words.
Each one has a thousand faces hidden under that blank expression,
and each one is asking you—and could care less what you reply—
something humble, something terrible: *Did you bring the key?*

Look, look: barren of melody or conception, these words
burrowed deep into the night.
Still damp and pregnant with sleep, they roll like rocks
down the harsh river and turn to scorn.

BlessBlessed
~ Patricia Smith

The burglar-barred church is warp, cardboard tilt, salvation
spiced and blotting the doorway. Amen to the little flailers,
stiff in pinafore and patent, scalps greased to glow, their

squirming buoyed by the adamant yowling of that organ
and best-sit-still glower from the elders—those dry baffling
women who bop synthetic cinnamon heads, tinny voices

dismantled and straining for the rafters. Pious knots, frayed
but holding, they will be lovingly unraveled by Jesus soon
enough. In spit-shined rooms doused in brocade, they pray

past Him in stunning rote, all vowing to be undone by
His wounds, His azure-eyed swoop, some stuff He said,
those hazy guide marks floundering in a confounding text.

This Sunday here, a real good Sunday. The rev is leaping,
threatening his natural spine, screeching of joy in the next
world: *Just no feeling like when the Lord brings you home*

then wraps His arms around you. Pews of the grizzled tingle.
Tambourines bang, ripple straight through to the backside,
Tony the organist stomps feral in his own sky, the choir sets

it sights on all those old bones. The Ghost shoves the agile
into the aisle. Stockings rip, matrons swirl, even the elders
rock in their seats when the reverend turns his lesson to fist:

You might not wake up tomorrow. You might not make it
home tonight. But think hard on what glory you got waitin'!
Service ends, or tries to, with a keen blaze lapping the walls.

From the basement wafts the siren stench of church supper—
chicken necks wilting in oil, collard greens, pork chops,
roasted yams rolled in brown sugar. Old folk groan gratitude,

say grace twice, slurp bounty from slow fingers, hiss hush
at those black obnoxious children. When they finally stand,
it is clearly an unfolding, pleats released and tumbling low

to brush brogans. Goodbye is *blessbless* and then the plod
from their church home to their own, passing storefronts
splintered behind padlock and link, walls scarred with names

of fallen children. No matter which way they trundle, drums
eke through dimming. Rude traffic buzzes their skin, the city
gets smaller. They think it's faith poking them forward through

ambling turn and turn, but it's the devil, Sunday gospel-drunk,
who guides them home. Tonight, again, he'll sit patiently by their
bedsides, clucking suggestively in the direction of their rest.

De Danaans, or Thank God for Plastic
~ Ron Smith

She told me they came in a great fleet
    to steal the land from the Fir Bolgs,
that on the western strands they set fire
       to their own boats. "No turning back,"
    she said, smirking—or maybe it was her version
of a leer. They believed the invaders
          had descended from a black cloud.
Out of the cloud they roared and the land
    bogged with blood. We were tossing back
      Manhattans in the Shelbourne Hotel.
She'd said she wanted to interview me

    about "the litrachur of the American Sooth."
"At Tara their Lia Fail shrieked," she said,
      when their first king settled himself
    onto the stone. "Dagda's cauldron
          fed them all. Their spears
and their swords pierced even rocks." I said
    something about Faulkner, about
Flannery getting the hell off the tracks.
    Nuada marched to Moytura and killed
Eochia Mac Erc and his one hundred thousand …
      Survivors splashed away

    in all directions to tiny islands. She
offered me, I'm not making this up, her cherry.
    At Tara, the victors circled
    their shrieking stone, chanting
thanks, chanting imprecations. We
    shook hands on the sidewalk, dry hand,
firm, with tiny bones. She hadn't taken a single note.

Maybe, I thought on my way down
Lower Baggott Street to sit beside snot-green Kavanagh
and stare with him at the scummy canal, maybe
she was wearing a wire.

White Deer
~ Lisa Russ Spaar

Have I fed too long on myth,
your quicksilver canthus shims,

vanquished pearl flank
in fractured scrim at day's close,

limning the charcoal grapevine
wicker, cochlear, blood-licked?

And live as much in your satin,
eroding shoal, elusive beyond garrison

fencing, caparisoned woods,
myrrh of squirrel, streaming traffic coals,

as I do here, in room-trapped
shadows run amok, menace

of bedstead, window sill, chair's lap?
If a truly cloistered nun, I might, to bind

gold-leaf to parchment
and—to touch—your topaz horns,

grind chalk on porphyry slab,
add mastic & just a blue, shop-cat's lick

of honey, checking its sweetness
with my own mouthed brush,

before applying the orient sadness,
oddly ebullient in this chaste text.

Root Canal
~ Maura Stanton

Sprawled in the dental chair while the surgeon
Probes the root of my tooth, I put myself
Back twenty years ago on a trail from St. Moritz.
I'm hiking Piz Nair, I'm not lying here
Bracing for the first needle, clenching my hands,
No, I'm looking up the steep incline at snow
Blocking my way though it's the end of June,
Snow, packed and shiny and slickly glistening—
Impossible to walk on without crampons.
I'll have to go *hors piste*, scramble sideways
Over rocks and rills. As the needle stings.
I bound from boulder to boulder, and land
In a pit of snow, clambering out, palms
Frozen and aching, my younger self determined
To reach the trail above me past the ice
Though this older self wants to turn around,
Forget the view of glaciers, distant peaks,
And go back down. A drill starts to vibrate.
I close my eyes against the surgeon's mask
And pant forward over roots, through drifts
Of soft wet snow sprinkled with pine needles,
Trying to circumvent the killer ice patch
By taking this other hard, but possible, route,
A crinkle-crankle route, my father called
Those twisty roads he drove as a salesman
Between farm towns, and now there's a moment
Without sound, without feeling—I look back
At the steeple in the valley far below me,
And then look up, I'm half-way to the point
Where I can rejoin the clear trail past the ice
Where Alpine flowers bloom, and birds sing,

And tourists picnic on cheese and chocolate,
If I'll only open wider, the surgeon says,
Open wider, that's it, just a little wider, thanks.

Excavations From The Tomb Of The Second Pharaoh, 12th Dynasty
~ Page Hill Starzinger

No, thanks
    I don't want to take the survey.
Patti Smith buried blue glass beads
        in an urn next to the headstone. Grave
        indeed.
    Do you deny yourself what you most want.
  If you don't interrupt   we can have a conversation.
What happened to self serve.
      Self-serving bias.

I just don't remember.

The young waxer touches me in a way I know she thinks I'm old.
    I recognize it because I
        touch my mother this way. This
is me. Stripped bare. A knee I don't know. A long back
that's familiar. A stranger's breast. How
do you settle
    in a body for so long,
        still want it to change. Still
it changes. Annotated legs, enlarged knuckles, skin tone muddied,
    some firm padding
  gone.   I ask the guard

        where Middle Kingdom is
      and he shows me.
Coffins with mummies tipped sideways, heads lined up with blue-
    rimmed eyes
  so they can see life
    through the casket.

Leg, lotus,
snails, snakes,
ankh.
resting-fold and
mellow low and
bleat.
Necklaces, so delicate,
amulets strung on thin
strings, lack of clasps. And they survive.

Boy on a Chair
~ Terese Svoboda

On parade with the dog doing her best,
we walk between two bodies of water,
not an island but wet blue ribbons

lapping land, and come upon a boy on a chair.
We do not have curbs on our lane so the chair
is where the lawn (such as sand permits)

begins, and the boy, who should be
at some screen, says *There!* and points
to what I've missed, head down with the dog:

the hot moon where our little tarmac
and the water rise up to link it,
suspended as if thrown and stuck

to a velcro black, its orange huge. Worship
is what the boy is doing, and the dog,
head lifted, begins to bark it.

To Be Tree
~ Brian Swann

> *O hoher Baum im ohr!*
> —Rilke, *Die Sonette an Orpheus*

I stand inside the white pine, braced against the trunk,
head a bird, hands needles, sometimes an hour or what
you call time when you can't count, ignored by what
or whatever, a planting, a co-tree, its consciousness

in human form, an inflected self hoping to become
what it is or feels itself to be but not to think of what it is,
just the last chance to turn away, back to where we once were,
fragrant, green, head a longing realized somewhere else,

all sense, a love focused, not to be a tree but not oneself,
no antecedent, no purpose, but desire that lay in wait until
it grew a tree to be in, looking out as a branch to touch air,
the world mediated as wind, leaving you as you were

but not the same, here where you can't lie down so
look up through the branches, here where you stand
in perspective, the height you need to know, so you
stand still and listen because in silence is more silence

and this you've come to hear, the hollow rich reverberations
all around where nothing happens, where the world opens
out to itself so you can go on forever, where there's
a tree surrounded by other trees but this is the tree

you want, the one you stand in as in a flame, and you
flare within it, no one would know the difference,
if they saw anything at all they would just see a tree,
they wouldn't see you, they wouldn't even look twice.

Wall
~ Brian Swann

A chipmunk dives into the old stone wall
I'm on, his home and harbor, taking

what's given, navigating crevices smooth
as air. I love him, the wall's lymph, its

voice—listen! flowing through everything,
calling you to find the ventriloquist so

you follow what you can't, through halls,
down corridors, by hanging gardens, onto

vistas he gives you opening onto new angles.
If souls exist, he's one.

from *Gave*
~ Cole Swensen

river. larger. larger in the sun.
                the river is wide. even farther.
to figure. the surface area of a river.
                a person with a compass
tracing perfect circles.
                it will be a finite number.
ending often. will be measured.
                if ever found the unit.
if ever stilled upon it
                the hand upon it counted:
one river two, two river three
                until new, a bend is turned
and I turned around
                and I looked back down
what looked like time—
                it was the way it moved in the sun
and the way the sun moved it.

from *Gave*
~ Cole Swensen

rising another river is a mist

suspended wind. in tiny

tiny pieces takes the air

apart in pieces

in linked digression with

links of spider web

silver-edged to the end of it

ended of it all

in which too are suspended

are lifted, the difference

between river and sky

hidden in the riding, who

was riding by.

from *Gave*
~ Cole Swensen

a river is a slippage
                is its business
                          river heading elsewhere
with a candle

river longer sideways than its description

            is its destination

                   flickers because there always is

a wind coming down the river

wavers. and all light wavers with it. a woman walking along it
holding out a lantern. a child walking along it, jumping from stone to
stone to stone in the dark. someone lights a match
it never reaches.

Under A Rising Moon
~ Arthur Sze

Driving at night between Chinle and Tsaile,
I fixate on deer along the road: in the headlights,
they're momentarily blinded but could leap out.
An unglazed pot fired and streaked from ash
will always bear the beauty of chance, while
a man who flies by helicopter and lands
on an iceberg will always recall the crunching
sounds under his feet. This morning I hiked
from the rim down to White House Ruins,
and the scraping of cottonwood leaves
is still in my ears. *Diné women tied their infants*
on cradleboards, stashed them in crevices
but never came back. Though warned of elk,
I heed the car with a single headlight enlarging
in my rearview mirror—when the mind
is sparked with pixels, it's hard to swerve
and brake. The Anasazi must have marveled
at the whitening sheen on the cliff, but tonight
tracks of moonlight run ahead of where I can be.

My Grandmother's Chores
~ Adam Tavel

Content with haste, I looped the bristle broom
back on its rung inside the laundry nook

and scampered off to Superman who sprawled
his glossy quests across the den. I liked

the way the comics slid across the room—
my carpet skis when, with a dash, I hooked

and soared across the plush before she called
from folding clothes to calm me down. What flights

I risked to mark my body's shadow frown
on imaginary Metropolis.

Pouting, I stacked a cover-crumpled pile.
Only then I heard the syncopated whisk

her labored sweeping made across the tiles
I fled to ride a city burning down.

Of Gods and Men and Monsters
~ Daniel Tobin

At the end of *Of Gods and Men* the monks
March side by side up a snowy mountain
Guarded by terrorists who will murder them
Off screen in the blinding grace of fog
Like a gas cloud, the stricken clutching cloth
As they do in *Gods and Monsters*—the flashback
Where James Whale, creator of *Frankenstein,*
The Bride of Frankenstein, Invisible Man, relives
The horrors endured in trench and redoubt.
The French Trappists who lived in Tibherine,
Their monastery nearby Islamic villagers
Who came to their door for aid, give their lives
To God, willing as they do to die for love,
For Christ would never abandon his flock
And they are each Christ, like the villagers
Who happen to believe a different history.
So terror incurs the way the monster
Wakes with the wrong brain, the criminal,
And not the original the master wished.
Such is the fallen world as the monks knew,
As their Master knew, and for love of which
He died. And for love of which, this world,
Stroke-ridden, mind flickering to its credits,
Whale, "the Queen of Hollywood," begins
His last flirtation with a hunky gardener—
"Put this gas mask on," the director orders,
As the young man poses nude, the mask
Making him a Minotaur, brute animal soul
Hiding at the center of the spiritual quest ...
Yes, the dying man's spurned, not unlike
His anguished creature, mute, taught to speak

By a blind hermit who too wants a friend—
Bread good, wine good—their Eucharistic meal,
Before the mob breaks in, before the Bride,
Her own body fashioned from scraps,
Screams in terror with one look at her mate;
Before Whale begs his friend to kill him
Before he kills himself which he does, his body
Floating mildly in the pool's stippled sunlight,
Like light rippling the flayed air of Tibherine...
One day he'll arrive at the door, the man
With the stylish fedora and bandaged face,
His whole body covered from head to toe
Under the fashionable overcoat and suit,
Wearing the goggles he'll remove to reveal
The missing eyes, the missing skull, before
He starts to unwind them, the bandages,
As if he was nothing but an un-healable wound.
And he is nothing, nothing, the nothing there,
Then a voice growing wilder with need,
Then the gone, gone in a rustle of bushes
Beyond the patio with the wind, as the creature
Stares from its lacework of scars—the creature
Muttering *Friend, friend* over again, the word
A puzzle, a questioning, while the hands,
Trembling, searching, the hastily sewn-on hands
Open for the offering, pleading again for love.

Aphrodite and the Flood
~ Marc Vincenz

for Pompeo Batoni

Evolution of a city
in perspective—

here in the longest night
windows are eyes.

They flicker half-alive.
Movement and flurries

over tinted rooftops,
then dusk & the painter resumes—

the moment is his fulcrum: drama
in the full face of the model

and the blush of her youth.
Circles whorled into ellipses

traced in empty space
and a kiss. A kiss

on the infant's brow.
Time, of course, is a variable:

the spurt of a plant
in its tangent, the acceleration

upon the slope,
the differential, then

the flux in the infinitesimal.
Such a slow process, to admire

the walls of the citadel
in their own passage

within the sacred
and the sometimes profane—

only this time when she poses
for her portrait, the bust of her

temperament endures
while watching the sun—

what a pastoral scene
cast in shadow, dying

within these four walls,
a symbol of her own

glazed over ice age.
But, I ask you this:

despite the migration of birds
and the planets hiding on her face,

how might she predict
the flood & the hurtling of the cannonball?

Genetic Drift, Common Sense, Allele Frequencies, Common Sense
~ Arthur Vogelsang

There are only two things God did not create,
The persistence of vision and the persistence of memory.
His first fire was followed instantly and I mean *instantly*
By His first rain, and in that *moment*, because He created such
A great smoke and a great rain, it was the two persistences' turn
And they passed Him unnoticed, in that small instant and I mean small—
God created a moment too small for himself to handle *anything*—
A God-tiny slice of a sec surrounded by thick smoke and thick rain,
These thick enough to create vaginas (leaf-covered) during their
Billowing and falling, among much else, yes, leaf-covered penises too—
Etcetera—stop signs and deer crossing signs for future highways for
Instance. So now the persistence of vision and the persistence
Of memory He's anxious about, or, well, we have to tell
The truth here or get zapped, He's afraid of them. They chip away at
Death each time a human does some persistence of vision and some
Persistence of memory, and there are many humans, more of them
As I and others have said alive now than all the dead counted together.
I have tried to do the two persistences voluntarily but, lucky
For God, it doesn't work that way, you can't stuff the ballot box
So to speak by doing your persistences over and over to try to
Freak God out. I will explain. The persistence of vision causes
Visual impressions to continue upon the retina for awhile,
And the persistence of memory causes impressions to continue
When you're not trying to remember them.
Wait a minute, isn't this unlucky for God?

Easy For Me
~ Connie Voisine

As easy as rasping the straw against the hole in the can,
without thinking, or thinking about some crap, easy
as chewing that straw, pressing plastic between teeth.
Then, look, my twisted dead root of a thing. Easy like that
foggy head feeling, the neighbor saying blah blah predicable
about kindness or the nothingness outside of god's love,
or the small, round mirror empty of lips, eyes, gray
part in the hair, easy because that mirror chips, dirties
until it's trashed in a slurry of purging—the photographs,
even the books you wrote, the thin silk slip, the ugly glare
in the stairway, the shoes with narrow heels, red sole,
            the button jar. Easy is the ruined after, the stagger,
the fidget, the mumbling, a vision of failing, worthlessness.
It's easy for me, to leave every night for a town where
I am the only one lost, for a hotel in which hunted animals
hang from the walls from some ancient idea of splendor,
and my weakness is apparent to a man, and no one I know
is still near. Easy for me, this tired face. My neighbor
told me that Judas wept afterward so much so that
his cheek had one deep wrinkle, a manifestation of
his grief for the consequences, his hatred of himself,
his eventual suicide. Hard to distinguish between
regret and self-hatred. Or it's easy for me to believe that.

Elegy for James Castle
~ G. C. Waldrep

I have not written about the bees
in months, it being winter.

Scratch this in spit and soot,
give it the head
of a chest of drawers, a hillside
caught on film.

Sew it with a thread of silk.

The bees, if they've survived,
dream deep in their winter hives.
I walk past them
the way a man walks
among tombs, that is,
with reverence, and some fear.

Not of what's inside,
but of what's guarding the chapel.

Because in the fairytales
none of us could hear, or speak.

The sky darkened
at odd hours of the day,
and the breeze freshened.
This was our interior,
our box alive with the familiar.

What I want to know most
is what you dreamed
of, when you were sleeping.

Because you must have slept,
although the authorities
keep their silence in this matter.

Freight Train Watches Me Do My Taiji
~ Afaa Michael Weaver

In the time the conveyors were down, the others
gone to lunch in the evening, in a quiet space along
the rolling ball bearings, the belts empty of boxes,

he sat on a pallet of soap waiting for a truck, sad
eyes in his blue uniform, nearly in tears sometimes
for reasons we never quite knew but could guess,

eyes that brightened and smiled when I did my Taiji,
a dance no one he knew knew how to do, no black man
for sure, only Chinese in books. I did the easier moves

at work, brush knee and twist, or repulse monkey,
which made him laugh, and I loved to make him laugh
when everyone else loved laughing at him in his pain,

his low place hovered over by angels who hanged
a saint's insignia over his head, a sign saved for folk
who suffered without knowing why, who sometimes

wanted to die in sadness. *Chug a chug, put a plug
in that sadness*, I would tell him to lift him up on days
he seemed to have fallen through all the circles of hell

to hit the bottom of suffering, a too full world in him.
I taught him the basics, and he memorized, took them
inside somewhere to a jewelry chest to keep safe,

I told him ancient stories like the one of masters
who came into this world to teach us in our dreams,
masters who could appear and disappear like angels,

and some days I quizzed him about the energies to see
how much he remembered. *Tell me the eight energies
again, Freight Train. I forgot.* He would chuckle,

roll all over from his waist to his shoulders and say
them in perfect order, *Ward off, rollback, press, push,
pluck, split, elbow, hip. You know what they is.*

We would laugh together, and one day he told me
he loved me, and to not fall apart I did the eight for him—
ward off, rollback, press, push, pluck, split, elbow, hip

until he laughed so hard the tears came back
as full as the child he had become in this world
with us where the world was too much for men

and men like me knew we had to leave. *You got
to be free*, he said on my last day as I walked away.
I looked back at the work where he had disappeared.

Slicker On
~ Scott Withiam

An orange Home Depot five-gallon bucket—
more than a few people depend on one
for what's encouraged. On its side,
going down in big white letters:
Let's DO This.

Let's. Inclusion,
there's a national bucket-load.
"Well, how are we doing?"
last night's wait person persisted,
but really she was pushing

for my order. "Look," I said, "*we're* fine,
but nationally, is there one side
you like best and might recommend?"
"They're all good," she said,
left and never returned.

Well, I liked this side: I walked out,
but *we* came along some anyway.
That's what I like about us, we come along
anyway. Even though the rain stopped,
our neighbor got out of *our* pickup

and put on *our* yellow slicker just so
our hands were free, so we could coax
our Home Depot bucket off the back
of our truck, leave it on our street and watch
our water slosh back and forth, back and forth,

while our black rubber hip-waders—
done wading, rolled down buccaneer-like—
swish-swashed against each other, against each other
all the way to our front door. Like pirates, *we,*
yet so unlike pirates we waded through our house,

turned on all of our lights
put on our favorite music, flopped
into our bed and fell into our sleep. La difference?
We slept with our slicker on.
Our yellow slicker under the lights left on

retained the persistent sheen of smelt
in the orange bucket—"Three or four races,"
the neighbor said last night, "not much
to bring home," which I just now included—
three to four smelt caught upstream mating,

slick in their own slurry, abandoned.
Sperm and eggs
because in the beginning beings want
to continue, and then: *they.* But we
couldn't forget that

this morning the rain came back,
and unlike those smelt we slipped out
of our back door without
changing. Hood up, slicker on,
we couldn't have come out any better prepared

for the day. And we held our head high,
as if we planned it that way.

Continuity
~ Geoffrey Young

What I have succeeded in saying to you
less a 20% introductory offer
starts about the premises and moves laterally
across the parking lot, finally working its way into roadside

brush before crashing into a thick pine forest. *Bonjour.*
But what of lips that having said their bit remain eloquent?
And what of all our selfish imperatives, reduced by sticky
laughter? A harsh wind soughs the heavy branches

of the hemlocks as I kiss the electronic nipple of American
kitsch goodbye. If only love made sense to me.
The science of painting may yet solve the mystery of art?
There's a name for the everything that the parts of everything

are a part of, but what is it? From this perch I harvest lobster
mushrooms on the lawn, plotting a stir-fry of nutty conviviality.

A Fleeting Hallucination
~ Sa'adi Youssef, translated by Marilyn Hacker

And because the rain
Has come to live on a hill in the suburbs
Inert
Durable
Erect
Like the garden gate or the doorway
Like the branch of a tree
You've begun to dream, awake, about the rain
A rain of roses fragmented into a drizzle
The rain of heavy drops
The rain of a wave soaking the shirts of shipwrecked sailors
The rain of the hurricane's tropical compassion
A rain you no longer have the power to hear
A rain of locusts
Rain in the veins of the country
A rain of ashes

Contributors' Biographies

Ekiwah Adler-Belendez is from Amatlan, Mexico, a small village an hour from Mexico City. The son of a North American father and a Mexican mother, Ekiwah is a poetic prodigy whose powerful verses have mesmerized Mexico's literary scene. Born September 14, 1987, Ekiwah is the author of three volumes of poetry: *Soy* (I Am); *Palabras Inagotables*, (Never-ending Words); *Weaver* (2003), his first book in English; and *The Coyote's Trace*, which features an introduction by Mary Oliver. Ekiwah lives in Massachusetts, has dual citizenship and is bilingual.

Kelli Russell Agodon is an award-winning poet, writer, and editor. She's the author of six books, most recently *Hourglass Museum* (Finalist for the Washington State Book Award in Poetry & the Julie Suk Poetry Prize) & *The Daily Poet: Day-By-Day Prompts For Your Writing Practice*. She is the co-founder of Two Sylvias Press, where she works as an editor and book cover designer. Her work has appeared in magazines such as *The Atlantic, New England Review*, and *O, The Oprah Magazine*. Kelli is also the Co-Director of the Poets on the Coast writing retreat as well as an avid paddleboarder, mountain biker, and hiker. She lives in a sleepy seaside town a ferry ride away from Seattle. agodon.com / twosylviaspress.com

Maram Al-Masri, a Franco-Syrian author and poet, was born in Lattakia-Syria and moved to France in 1982 following the completion of English Literature studies at Damascus University. Her first poetry collection, *I Threaten You with a White Dove*, was published in 1987. Her second collection, *A Red Cherry on a White-Tiled Floor*, was published in Tunisia by l'Or du Temps Editions in 1997, and in French translation by Éditions PHA in 2003. It was also translated into English by Khaled Mattawa and published in a bilingual edition in 2004 by Bloodaxe Books. In 2007 Al Manar released *I Look at You*, which was awarded the Prix d'Automne 2007 de Poésie de la Société des Gens De Lettres in Paris.

She received the Adonis Prize of the Lebanese Cultural Forum in 1998, the Premio Citta di Calopezzati for the section Poésie de la Mediterranée, and Il Fiore d'Argento 2015. She was recently awarded the 5th Dante Alighieri Prize. Other works include the poetry collections *Le retour de walada, Par la fontaine de ma bouche, La robe froissée, Elle va nue la liberté, Le rapt,* and two anthologies, including *Femmes poètes du monde arabe.*

Sandra Alcosser's poems have appeared in *The New Yorker, The New York Times, Paris Review, Ploughshares, Poetry,* and the *Pushcart Prize Anthology.* She received two individual artist fellowships from National Endowment for the Arts, and her books of poetry, *A Fish to Feed All Hunger* and *Except by Nature,* received the highest honors from National Poetry Series, Academy of American Poets and Associated Writing Programs, as well as the Larry Levis Award and the William Stafford Award for Poetry. Her four artist book collaborations with Brighton Press have been exhibited internationally and reside in museum and special collections including The National Museum of Women in the Arts and Musee d'Art Americain–Giverny. She was the National Endowment for the Arts' first Conservation Poet for the Wildlife Conservation Society and Poets House, New York, as well as Montana's first poet laureate and recipient of the Merriam Award for Distinguished Contribution to Montana Literature. She founded and directs SDSU's MFA program each fall and teaches with Pacific University's low-residency MFA program.

Meena Alexander's seventh book of poetry is *Birthplace with Buried Stones* (TriQuarterly Books/ Northwestern University Press, 2013) Her works include Illiterate Heart, winner of the PEN Open Book Award and *Quickly Changing River* (both published by TriQuarterly Books/ Northwestern University Press). She is the author of the critically acclaimed memoir *Fault Lines* (one of Publishers Weekly's Best Books of the Year) and editor of *Indian Love Poems* (Knopf/ Everyman's Library). Her poems have been widely translated and set to music. She has received awards from the John Simon Guggenheim Foundation, the Fulbright and Rockefeller Foundations, the ACLS and the Arts Council of England. meenaalexander.com

Nin Andrews is the author of twelve collections of poetry including *The Book of Orgasms, Sleeping with Houdini*, and her latest book, *Why God Is a Woman*. The recipient of two Ohio Arts Council grants, her poems have appeared in many literary reviews and anthologies including *Ploughshares, The Paris Review, The Best of the Prose Poem*, and four volumes of *Best American Poetry*.

Ralph Angel's latest book is *Your Moon* (New Issues, 2014). He lives in Los Angeles.

Robert Archambeau's books include the collections of poetry *Home and Variations* (Salt) and *The Kafka Sutra* (MadHat) and the studies *Laureates and Heretics* (Notre Dame) and *The Poet Resigns: Poetry in a Difficult World* (Akron). He is also the editor of three books: *Word Play Place: Essays on the Poetry of John Matthias* (Ohio/Swallow), *Letters of Blood and Other English Writings of Goran Printz-Pahlson* (Open Book) and *The &NOW Awards: The Best Innovative Writing* (&NOW). He teaches at Lake Forest College.

Rae Armantrout's new and selected poems, *Partly*, is coming out from Wesleyan in the fall of 2016. She has published eleven books of poetry and has also been featured in a number of major anthologies. Her book of poems *Versed* was awarded the 2009 National Book Critics Circle Award and the 2010 Pulitzer Prize for Poetry. Armantrout's most recent collection is *Itself*.

Simon Armitage is the current Professor of Poetry at Oxford University.

Sally Ball is the author of *Annus Mirabilis* and *Wreck Me*, both from Barrow Street. She is an associate professor of English at Arizona State University and also an associate director of Four Way Books.

Benno Barnard writes in Dutch. *A Public Woman*, a selection of his poetry in a translation by David Colmer, was published by Eyewear Publishing, London, in 2015.

Ellen Bass's poetry has appeared in *The New Yorker, The New York Times Magazine*, and *American Poetry Review*. Her books include *Like a Beggar, The Human Line*, and *Mules of Love*. She co-edited the groundbreaking *No More Masks! An Anthology of Poems by Women*, and her nonfiction books include *Free Your Mind: The Book for Gay, Lesbian and Bisexual Youth* and *The Courage to Heal*. She has received a Fellowship from the National Endowment for the Arts, two Pushcart Prizes, The Lambda Literary Award and many other honors. She teaches in the MFA program at Pacific University.

Charles Baxter is the author most recently of *There's Something I Want You to Do* (February 2015), and *Gryphon: New and Selected Stories* (2011). His third novel, *The Feast of Love*, was a finalist for the National Book Award in 2000. He has authored a book of poetry: *Imaginary Paintings: And Other Poems*. He has received the Award of Merit in the Short Story and the Award in Literature from the American Academy of Arts and Letters. His work has appeared in *The New Yorker, The Atlantic, The New York Review of Books* and *Harper's*, among others. He lives in Minneapolis and is currently the Edelstein Keller Professor of Creative Writing at the University of Minnesota.

Robin Behn's most recent collection is *The Yellow House*. She directs the MFA Program in Creative Writing at the University of Alabama and is working on the libretto of a new opera about the burning of that campus during the last days of the Civil War.

April Bernard's fifth collection of poems, *Brawl & Jag*, will be published by W. W. Norton in March 2016. She frequently writes for *The New York Review of Books*, teaches in the Bennington MFA program, and is Professor of English at Skidmore College.

Charles Bernstein's *Pitch of Poetry*, new essays, will be out in spring 2016 from University of Chicago Press. His most recent book of poems is *Recalculating* (Chicago, 2013). In 2015 Bernstein was awarded both the Münster Prize for International Poetry and Janus Pannonius Grand Prize for Poetry. More info at epc.buffalo.edu.

Linda Bierds is the author of nine volumes of poetry, most recently *Roget's Illusion*, which was longlisted for the 2014 National Book Award. Her work appears regularly in *The Atlantic*. She has won several major awards and grants including the Guggenheim and the "genius" grant from the MacArthur Foundation.

Sally Bliumis-Dunn teaches Modern Poetry at Manhattanville College and the Palm Beach Poetry Festival. Her poems have appeared in *New Ohio Review, The Paris Review, Prairie Schooner, Poetry London, The Bellevue Literary Review, The New York Times, PBS NewsHour, Terrain, The Writer's Almanac*, The Academy of American Poets' Poem-a-day, and Ted Kooser's newspaper column, among others. In 2002, she was a finalist for the Nimrod/Hardman Pablo Neruda Prize. Her third book, *Echolocation*, is currently seeking a publishing home.

Yves Bonnefoy, often acclaimed as France's greatest living poet, has published nine major collections of verse, several books of tales, and numerous studies of literature and art. He has also served as the chief editor of an important dictionary of world mythology, in two volumes. He succeeded Roland Barthes in the Chair of Comparative Poetics at the Collège de France, and is perennially cited as a leading candidate for the Nobel Prize for Literature. His work has been translated into scores of languages, and he himself is a celebrated translator of Shakespeare, Yeats, Keats, and Leopardi. Most recently, he has added the European Prize for Poetry of 2006 and the Kafka Prize for 2007 to his long list of honors. He lives in Paris.

Marianne Boruch is the author of eight poetry collections, most recently *Cadaver, Speak* and *The Book of Hours*, a Kingsley-Tufts Poetry

Award winner, both from Copper Canyon Press. Her ninth book, *Eventually One Dreams the Real Thing*, is due out from CCP in 2016. Her work has appeared in *The New Yorker, Poetry, London Review of Books, American Poetry Review, The Nation, The New York Review of Books* and elsewhere. Her awards include fellowships from the NEA and the Guggenheim Foundation. She's been a Fulbright Professor at the University of Edinburgh and had artist residencies at Bellagio, the American Academy in Rome, at Yaddo, the Anderson Center, and MacDowell, and at national parks Denali and Isle Royale. She teaches in the MFA programs at Purdue University and Warren Wilson College.

David Bottoms' first book, *Shooting Rats at the Bibb County Dump* (William Morrow, 1980), was chosen by Robert Penn Warren as winner of the 1979 Walt Whitman Award of the Academy of American Poets. His poems have appeared widely in magazines such as *The Atlantic, The New Yorker, Harper's, Poetry*, and *The Paris Review*, as well as in sixty anthologies and textbooks. He is the author of seven other books of poetry, two novels, and a book of essays and interviews, including *We Almost Disappear* (Copper Canyon Press, 2011).

Daniel Bourne's books of poetry include *The Household Gods* (Cleveland State University Press, 1995), *Where No One Spoke the Language* (CustomWords, 2006) and a collection of translations of the Polish political poet Tomasz Jastrun, *On the Crossroads of Asia and Europe* (Salmon Run, 1999). He teaches in the English Department and Environmental Studies at the College of Wooster, where he edits *Artful Dodge*. His many trips to Poland include a graduate fellowship between Indiana University and Warsaw University in 1982–83 and a Fulbright fellowship in 1985–87 for the translation of younger Polish poets. His poems have appeared in such journals as *Ploughshares, FIELD, Guernica, American Poetry Review, Prairie Schooner, Shenandoah, Salmagundi, Tar River Poetry*, and *Cimarron Review*. His translations of other Polish poets such as Bronisław Maj and Zbigniew Machej appear in *FIELD, Boulevard, Mid-American Review, Virginia Quarterly Review*, and elsewhere. In July 2013, *Plume* printed as its Special Feature his translations of another Polish poet, "The Angel's Share: Six Poems by Krzysztof Kuczkowski." Finally, "Agitprop" and "To the Feral Cats of Vilnius," two of Bourne's poems from his collection *Where No One Spoke the Language* and originally appearing in *Salmagundi*, will be reprinted in a special issue celebrating that journal's 50th anniversary in the coming year.

Julie Bruck is the author of three books of poetry, most recently *Monkey Ranch* (Brick Books, 2012). Her work has appeared in *Ms., Ploughshares, Numero Cinq, The New Yorker*, and many other journals and magazines. She was the recipient of Canada's 2012 Governor General's Literary Award for Poetry.

Christopher Buckley's *Star Journal: Selected Poems* will be published by the U. of Pittsburgh Press in fall 2016. His twentieth book of poetry, *Back Room at the Philosophers' Club*, was published in 2014 by Stephen F. Austin State U. Press. Among several critical collections and anthologies of contemporary poetry, he has edited *A Condition of the Spirit: The Life and Work of Larry Levis*, 2004, with Alexander Long; *Bear Flag Republic: Prose Poems and Poetics from California*, 2008; and *One for the Money: The Sentence as a Poetic Form*, from Lynx House Press, 2012, both with Gary Young. He has also edited *On the Poetry of Philip Levine: Stranger to Nothing*, U. of Michigan Press 1991, *First Light: A Festschrift for Philip Levine on his 85th Birthday*, 2013, and *Messenger to the Stars: A Luis Omar Salinas New Selected Poems & Reader* for Tebot Bach's Ash Tree Poetry Series, Fall 2014

Cathleen Calbert's poetry, short fiction, and creative nonfiction have appeared in many publications, including *The New Republic, The New York Times, The Paris Review, Poetry*, and *The Women's Review of Books*. She is the author of three books of poetry: *Lessons in Space* (University of Florida Press), *Bad Judgment* (Sarabande Books), and *Sleeping with a Famous Poet* (C.W. Books). Her awards include *The Nation* Discovery Award, a Pushcart Prize, and the Tucker Thorp Professorship at Rhode Island College, where she currently teaches.

Peter Campion is the author of three collections of poems, *Other People, The Lions,* and *El Dorado,* all from the University of Chicago Press. He directs the creative writing program at the University of Minnesota.

Hélène Cardona is a poet, literary translator and actor, the recipient of numerous awards and honors including a Hemingway Grant and the USA Best Book Award. Her books include two translations: *Beyond Elsewhere* and *Ce que nous portons*; and three bilingual poetry collections, most recently *Life in Suspension* and *Dreaming My Animal Selves.* She also translated Walt Whitman's *Civil War Writings* for the Iowa International Writing Program's *WhitmanWeb.*

She co-edits *Fulcrum: An Anthology of Poetry and Aesthetics,* is Essay contributor to *The London Magazine,* and co-producer of the documentary *Pablo Neruda: The Poet's Calling.* She holds a Master's in American Literature from the Sorbonne, taught at Hamilton College & Loyola Marymount University, and received fellowships from the Goethe-Institut & Universidad Internacional de Andalucía. Publications include *Washington Square, World Literature Today, Poetry International, The Irish Literary Times, The Warwick Review, TAB: The Journal of Poetry & Poetics,* and elsewhere.

Maxine Chernoff chairs the Creative Writing Program at SFSU and is former editor of New American Writing. She has published 14 books of poetry and is the winner of a poetry NEA in 2013 and of the 2009 PEN Translation award for her co-translation of the German poet Friedrich Hoelderlin. Her most recent book of poems is *Here* (Counterpath, 2014), finalist for the Northern California Book Award.

Patricia Clark is a professor in the Writing Department and also the poet-in-residence at Grand Valley State University in Michigan Her poetry has appeared in magazines such as *The Atlantic, Poetry, Slate, New England Review, North American Review, Pennsylvania Review, Black Warrior Review,* and *Seattle Review.* She is the recipient of a Creative Artist Grant from ArtServe Michigan for 2003. Her book of poems *North of Wondering* won the first book competition sponsored by Women in Literature, Inc. Patricia has also co-edited an anthology of contemporary women writers, *Worlds in Our Words*. Her most recent book of poems is *Sunday Rising* (2013).

Andrea Cohen's poems have appeared in *The New Yorker, The Atlantic, Poetry, Threepenny Review*, and elsewhere. Her fifth poetry collection, *Unfathoming*, is forthcoming from Four Way Books. Other recent collections include *Furs Not Mine* and *Kentucky Derby*. She directs the Writers House at Merrimack College and the Blacksmith House Poetry Series in Cambridge, MA.

Peter Cole's recent books of poems include *The Invention of Influence* (New Directions) and *The Poetry of Kabbalah: Mystical Verse from the Jewish Tradition* (Yale). In the spring of 2017 FSG will publish *Hymns & Qualms: New and Selected Poems and Translations*. A 2007 MacArthur Fellow, Cole divides his time between Jerusalem and New Haven.

Billy Collins' latest collection is *Aimless Love: New and Selected Poems* (Random House, 2013). He is a Distinguished Professor at Lehman College (CUNY) and a Senior Distinguished Fellow of the Winter Park Institute at Rollins College. He served as United States Poet Laureate 2001–2003.

Martha Collins' eighth book of poems, *Admit One: An American Scrapbook*, was published by Pittsburgh in 2016. Collins is also the author of seven earlier books of poetry, most recently *Day Unto Day, White Papers*, and *Blue Front*, and co-translator of four collections of Vietnamese poetry. She is editor-at-large for *FIELD* magazine and an editor for the Oberlin College Press.

David Colmer is an Australian translator, mainly of Dutch-language literature, and the winner of numerous translation awards. His translation of a selection of Benno Barnard's poetry, *A Public Woman*, was published by Eyewear Publishing in 2015. His translation of Nachoem M. Wijnberg's *Divan of Ghalib* is due out with White Pine Press in early 2016.

Peter Cooley's latest book of poetry is *Night Bus to the Afterlife*. Recent poems have appeared in *Southern Review, The Hopkins Review, The Other Journal*, and *Conte*. He is Senior Mellon Professor in the Humanities and Director of Creative Writing at Tulane, and Louisiana Poet Laureate.

Tom Crawford is a teacher and poet whose work explores the natural world and our complex connection to it. Born in Michigan and educated in California, he's lived much of his life in the Northwest. Years of teaching in China and South Korea have infused his work with a quality of Eastern sensibility. His poems are both contemplative and activist. They're not just about beauty but how to save it. *Caging the Robin*, his latest book, came out in December 2014. Recent presentations: Yosemite National Park and the Mono Lake Bird Chautauqua in Lee Vining, CA. In September 2015 he was guest speaker at Auburn University for the installation *The Art of Vanishing* in celebration of Audubon's life and work. He's the author of seven books of poetry: *Lauds* won the Oregon Book Award; *The Temple On Monday* was winner of the ForeWord Book of the Year Award; and *The Names of Birds*, his last collection, star-reviewed in BookList, has become a favorite among bird watchers in America. He's the recipient of the Pushcart Prize, and two National Endowments for the Arts Fellowship.

Cynthia Cruz the author of three collections of poems: *Ruin*, published by Alice James Books in 2006, *The Glimmering Room*, published by Four Way Books in 2012, and *Wunderkammer*, her third collection, was published by Four Way Books in 2014. Her fourth collection, *How the End Begins*, also from Four Way Books, is forthcoming in 2016. Her essays and art writings have been published in *The Los Angeles Review of Books, American Poetry Review, Guernica*, and *The Rumpus*. She is also currently at work on two poetry anthologies: one of Latina poets and the other, a collection of poetry by female poets around the issue of consumption and nourishment. A regular contributor for the art journal *Hyperallergic*, she is currently at work on a collection of essays on language and iterations of silence.

Jim Daniels' recent publications include the chapbook, *Apology to the Moon* (BatCat Press, 2015), *Eight Mile High*, stories (Michigan State University Press, 2014) and *Birth Marks*, poems (BOA Editions, 2013). *The End of Blessings*, a short film he wrote and produced, is currently making the rounds of film festivals, and his poems and the photographs of Charlee Brodsky, previously featured in *Plume*, are on display in their show *Beyond the Obvious* at the Robert Morris University Art Gallery. Daniels is the Thomas Stockham Baker University Professor at Carnegie Mellon University.

Kwame Dawes is the author of nineteen books of poetry and numerous other books of fiction, criticism, and essays. He has edited over a dozen anthologies. His most recent collection, *City of Bones* (Northwestern University Press) will appear in 2016 along with *Speak from Here to There*, a co-written collection of verse with Australian poet John Kinsella, and *A Bloom of Stones*, a tri-lingual anthology of Haitian poetry written after the earthquake, which he edited. A Spanish-language collection of his poems, titled *Vuelo*, will appear in Mexico in 2016. He is Glenna Luschei Editor of *Prairie Schooner* and teaches at the University of Nebraska and the Pacific MFA Program. He is Director of the African Poetry Book Fund and Artistic Director of the Calabash International Literary Festival.

Carl Dennis is the author of twelve books of poems, most recently *Another Reason* (Penguin, 2014). A recipient of the Pulitzer Prize and the Ruth Lilly Prize, he lives in Buffalo, New York.

W. S. Di Piero is the author of many books of poetry, essays, and translations. His recent books of poems are *Nitro Nights* (Copper Canyon, 2011) and *TOMBO* (McSweeney's, 2014); his recent essay collections are *City Dog* and *When Can I See you Again: New Art Writings*. He's a frequent contributor to *Threepenny Review* and writes a regular column on the visual arts for an independent weekly newspaper, *The San Diego Reader*. He lives in San Francisco.

Norman Dubie is the author of twenty-five books of poetry, most recently *Quotations of Bone* (2015). His other books of poetry include *The Volcano* (2010), *The Insomniac Liar of Topo* (2007), *Ordinary Mornings of a Coliseum* (2004), and *The Mercy Seat* (2001), all from Copper Canyon Press. He is the recipient of the Bess Hokin Prize from the Poetry Foundation, the PEN Center USA Literary Award for Poetry in 2002, and fellowships and grants from the Ingram Merrill Foundation, the John Simon Guggenheim Memorial Foundation, and the National Endowment for the Arts. He lives and teaches in Tempe, AZ.

Denise Duhamel's most recent book of poetry, *Blowout* (University of Pittsburgh Press, 2013), was a finalist for the National Book Critics Circle Award. Her other titles include *Ka-Ching!* (Pittsburgh, 2009), *Two and Two* (Pittsburgh, 2005), *Queen for a Day: Selected and New Poems* (Pittsburgh, 2001), *The Star-Spangled Banner* (winner of the Crab Orchard Award, SIU Press, 1999) and *Kinky* (Orchises Press, 1997). Her work with Maureen Seaton was published in *CAPRICE* (Collaborations: Collected, Uncollected, and New) by Sibling Rivalry Press in 2015. The recipient of fellowships from the Guggenhiem Foundation and the National Endowment for the Arts, Duhamel is a professor at Florida International University in Miami.

Efe Duyan (b. 1981, İstanbul, Turkey), studied architecture and philosophy in Middle East Technical University (BA), History and Theory of Architecture in Yıldız Technical University (MS) and History of Architecture in Mimar Sinan Fine Arts University (Ph.D.). He is currently teaching history of architecture as an assitnat professor at Mimar Sinan Fine Arts University. As a poet he has been invited to several workshops, readings and international organizations including Word-Express Project, Edinburgh Book Festival, London Book Fair, Berlin Poetry Festival, Lodeve Poetry Festival, Riga Poetry Days, Malta İnizjamed Poetry Festival and Transylvania Poetry Poetry Festival. Some of his poems have been translated into Bosnian, Czech, Chinese, Croatian, Danish, English, Estonian, French, Greek, German, Hebrew, Hungarian, Italian, Latvian, Lithuanian, Rumanian, Macedonian,

Maltese, Occitan, Slovenian, Ukrainian and Welsh. His translations include poetry collections of Radu Vancu (Romania), Matthias Göritz (Germany) and Lloyd Schwartz (USA). He edited a comtemporary poetry anthology, *Bir Benden Bir O'ndan* (2010) and is on the editorial board of the literature magazine *Istanbul Offline*. His critical essay "The Construction of Characters in Nâzım Hikmet's Poetry" was been published in 2008. His poetry collections are *Sıkça Sorulan Sorular* (Frequently Asked Questions, 2016), *Tek Şiirlik Aşklar* (One Poem Stands, 2012) and *Takas* (Barter, 2006).

Born in Gdańsk in 1953, **Tadeusz Dziewanowski** was involved in Polish street theater as both a writer and performer during the 1970s, and was a co-founder of the Gdansk-area creative group, Tawerna Psychonautow (The Tavern of the Psychonauts) in the 1980s. More recently, he has been a poet and translator from English. His first book of poetry, *Siedemnaście tysięcy małpich ogonów* (Seventeen Thousand Monkey Tales), appeared in 2009, and his poetry, reviews and translations from English appear regularly in the major Polish literary journal *Topos*. In the U.S., Daniel Bourne's translations of his poetry have previously appeared in *Plume*, *International Poetry Review*, and *Cerise Press*.

Cornelius Eady, poet and co-founder of Cave Canem, has published more than half a dozen volumes of poetry, among them *Victims of the Latest Dance Craze* (1985), winner of the Lamont Poetry Prize from the Academy of American Poets; *The Gathering of My Name* (1991), nominated for a Pulitzer Prize; and *Brutal Imagination* (2001), a National Book Award finalist. His work in theater includes the libretto for an opera, *Running Man*, which was a finalist for the Pulitzer Prize in Drama in 1999. His play *Brutal Imagination* won *Newsday's* Oppenheimer award.

Lynn Emanuel is the author of five books of poetry, *Hotel Fiesta* (University of Georgia Press,1984), *The Dig* (University of Illinois Press, 1992), *Then, Suddenly—* (University of Pittsburgh Poetry Series, 1999), *Noose and Hook* (University of Pittsburgh Poetry Series, 2010), and, most recently, *The Nerve Of It : Poems New and Selected* (University of Pittsburgh Poetry Series, 2015). Her work has been featured in the *Pushcart Prize Anthology* and *Best American Poetry* numerous times and is included in *The Oxford Book of American Poetry* and the Norton anthology of American hybrid poetry. Most recently her poetry has been published in the *New York Times* and is forthcoming in *Best American Poetry, 2016.* She has been a judge for the National Book Awards and has taught at the Bread Loaf Writers' Conference, The Warren Wilson Program in Creative Writing, and the Bennington College Low Residency MFA program. Among the awards she has received are two fellowships from the National Endowment for the Arts, The National Poetry Series Award, the Eric Matthieu King Award from The Academy of American Poets and, most recently, a fellowship to the Ranieri Foundation.

Elaine Equi's books include *Ripple Effect: New & Selected Poems, Click and Clone*, and, most recently, *Sentences and Rain*, all from Coffee House Press. She lives in New York City and teaches at New York University and in the MFA program at The New School.

Kathleen Flenniken's two poetry collections are *Plume* (University of Washington, 2012), a finalist for the William Carlos Williams Award from the Poetry Society of America, and *Famous* (University of Nebraska, 2006) which was an ALA Notable Book and winner of the *Prairie Schooner* Book Prize.

Stuart Friebert's *Floating Heart* won the Ohioana Poetry Award for 2015. His new book, *On the Bottom*, is just out (Iris Press), as is his tenth collection of translations, *Be Quiet: Selected Poems of Kuno Raeber* (Tiger Bark Press)

Jeff Friedman has published six poetry collections, five with Carnegie Mellon University Press, including *Pretenders* (2014), *Working in Flour* (2011), and *Black Threads* (2008). His poems, mini stories and translations have appeared in many literary magazines, including

American Poetry Review, Poetry, New England Review, The Antioch Review, Poetry International, Hotel Amerika, Vestal Review, Quick Fiction, Flash Fiction Funny, Smokelong Quarterly, Prairie Schooner, 100-Word Story, Solstice, Storyscape, Journal of Compressed Creative Arts, and *The New Republic.* Dzvinia Orlowsky's and his translation of *Memorials* by Polish poet Mieczsław Jastrun was published by Lavender Ink/Dialogos in August 2014. He and Orlowsky were awarded an NEA Literature Translation Fellowship for 2016.

Four Pushcart Prize anthologies have published poems by **Carol Frost**, as wall as *Poetry, Shenendoah, Gettysburg Review, The Atlantic, The New York Times, Subtropics,* and *Kenyon Review;* poems forthcoming in The *New Republic* and an essay on Wallace Stevens in *New England Review. Entwined: Three Lyric Sequences,* her twelfth collection, appeared in 2014 from Tupelo Press. She teaches at Rollins College, where she is the Theodore Bruce and Barbara Lawrence Alfond Professor of English and she directs Winter with the Writers, a yearly literary festival.

Jean-Luc Garneau is a linguist and the author of two books: *Semantic Divergence in Anglo-French Cognates: A Synchronic Study in Contrastive Lexicography* (Jupiter Press) and *La rivière des morts* (La Plume d'Oie Edition), a collection of poems and stories. He lives in Chicago.

Sandra M. Gilbert has published eight collections of poetry and among prose books *Wrongful Death, Death's Door, Rereading Women,* and most recently *The Culinary Imagination: From Myth to Modernity.* She is currently at work on a new collection of poems, *Saturn's Meal,* and on *Eating Words,* an anthology of food writing coedited by Roger Porter. With Susan Gubar, she is coauthor of *The Madwoman in the Attic* and other works: the two received the 2012 Award for Lifetime Achievement from the National Book Critics Circle.

Ani Gjika is an Albanian-American poet, literary translator, and author of *Bread on Running Waters* (Fenway Press, 2013), a finalist for the 2011 Anthony Hecht Poetry Prize and 2011 May Sarton

New Hampshire Book Prize. Her other honors include awards and fellowships from the National Endowment for the Arts, the Robert Pinsky Global Fellowship, the Banff Centre International Literary Translators Residency and the Robert Fitzgerald Translation Prize. Gjika's own poetry appears in *Seneca Review, Salamander, From the Fishouse* and elsewhere. Her translations from the Albanian appear in *World Literature Today, Ploughshares, AGNI Online, Catamaran Literary Reader, Two Lines Online, From the Fishouse* and elsewhere.

Beckian Fritz Goldberg received her MFA in 1985 from Vermont College and is the author of seven volumes of poetry, *Body Betrayer* (Cleveland State University Press, 1991,) *In the Badlands of Desire* (Cleveland State University, 1993,) *Never Be the Horse*, winner of the University of Akron Poetry Prize (University of Akron Press, 1999), *Twentieth-Century Children*, a limited edition chapbook, winner of the *Indiana Review* chapbook prize (Graphic Design Press, Indiana University, 1999), *Lie Awake Lake*, winner of the 2004 FIELD Poetry Prize (Oberlin College Press, 2005,) *The Book of Accident* (University of Akron Press, 2006,) *Reliquary Fever: New and Selected Poems* (New Issues Press, 2010) and *Egypt From Space* (Oberlin, 2013.) Goldberg has been awarded the Theodore Roethke Poetry Prize from *Poetry Northwest, The Gettysburg Review* Annual Poetry Prize, two Arizona Commission on the Arts Poetry Fellowships (1993, 2001) and two Pushcart Prizes. Her work has appeared in numerous anthologies such as *New American Poets of the '90s, Best American Poetry 1995, American Alphabets: 25 Contemporary Poets, Best American Poetry 2011, Best American Poetry 2013* and in journals, including *American Poetry Review, FIELD, The Gettysburg Review, Harper's, The Iowa Review, Michigan Quarterly Review, Gulf Coast*, and many others. She currently lives in Arizona.

Marilyn Hacker is the author of thirteen books of poems, including *A Stranger's Mirror* (W. W. Norton, 2015), *Names* (W. W. Norton, 2010) and *Desesperanto* (W. W. Norton, 2003), an essay collection, *Unauthorized Voices* (Michigan, 2010), and thirteen collections of translations of French and Francophone poets including Emmanuel

Moses, Marie Etienne, Vénus Khoury-Ghata, Habib Tengour and Rachida Madani. *DiaspoRenga*, a collaborative sequence written with the Palestinian-American poet Deema Shehabi, was published by Holland Park Press in 2014. Her awards include the Lenore Marshall Prize in 1995 for *Winter Numbers*, two Lambda Literary Awards, the 2009 PEN award for poetry in translation, the 2010 PEN Voelcker Award and the international Argana Prize for Poetry from the Beit as-Sh'ir/ House of Poetry in Morocco in 2011. She lives in Paris.

Rachel Hadas is Board of Governors Professor of English at Rutgers-Newark. Her book of prose, *Talking to the Dead*, was published in 2015 by Spuyten Duyvil Press; a new book of poems, *Questions in the Vestibule*, will be published in April 2016 by Northwestern University Press. Her translations of Euripides' plays *Iphigenia in Aulis* and *Iphigenia among the Taurians* will also be published by Northwestern University Press.

Barbara Hamby's newest book is *On the Street of Divine Love: New And Selected Poems*, from the Pitt Poetry Series.

Allison Adelle Hedge Coke's books include *Streaming, Blood Run, Off-Season City Pipe, Dog Road Woman, Sing: Poetry from the Indigenous Americas, Effigies, Effigies II*, and *Rock, Ghost, Willow, Deer*. Awards include an American Book Award, a King*Chavez*Parks Award, Lifetime Achievement Award, 2015, Native Writers Circle of the Americas, a 2015 Pen Southwest Book Award, and a 2016 Library of Congress Witter Bynner Fellowship. She teaches for VCFA MFA in Writing & Publishing, Red Earth MFA, and as Visiting Writer for SWP Naropa.

John Hennessy is the author of two collections, *Coney Island Pilgrims* and *Bridge and Tunnel*, and his poems appear in many journals and anthologies, including *Best American Poetry 2013, The Believer, Poetry, Fulcrum, Harvard Review, The New Republic, The Huffington Post, Best New Poets 2005*, and *The Yale Review*. Hennessy went to Princeton

University on a Cane Scholarship, and he received graduate degrees from the University of Texas at Austin and the University of Arkansas. In 2007–2008 he held the Resident Fellowship in Poetry at the Amy Clampitt House. Hennessy is the poetry editor of *The Common*, a print magazine based at Amherst College, and teaches at the University of Massachusetts–Amherst.

W. N. Herbert (born 1961) is a poet from Dundee, Scotland. He writes in both English and Scots. He and Richard Price founded the poetry magazine *Gairfish*. In 1994, he was one of 20 poets chosen by a panel of judges as the New Generation in a promotion organised by the Poetry Society. He became a Professor of Poetry & Creative Writing at the University of Newcastle, and in September 2013, Herbert was appointed as Dundee's first makar. He became a Fellow of the Royal Society of Literature in 2015. His poetry books are *Dundee Doldrums* (1991), *The Testament of the Reverend Thomas Dick* (1994), *Cabaret McGonagall* (1996), *The Laurelude* (1998), *The Big Bumper Book of Troy* (2002), *Bad Shaman Blues* (2006), *Omnesia* (2013).

Bob Hicok's latest book, *Elegy Owed* (Copper Canyon, 2013), was a finalist for the National Book Critics Circle Award. *Sex & Love &* will be published by Copper Canyon in 2016.

Tony Hoagland's four collections of poems include *What Narcissism Means to Me* and *Donkey Gospel*. A new book of essays on poetic craft and art, *Twenty Poems That Could Save America*, has just been published by Graywolf Press. He teaches at the University of Houston and also at the Warren Wilson low-residency MFA. In 2012, he started Five Powers of Poetry, a program for coaching high school teachers in the teaching of poetry in the classroom.

Michael Hofmann is a poet and translator from the German (poetry and prose). His most recent publications are *Where Have You Been?* (FSG) a book of essays, and a selection of Joseph Roth's journalism called *The Hotel Years* (New Directions). He teaches at the University of Florida.

T. R. Hummer's twelfth book of poems, *Eon*—which completes a three-book project ten years in the making—will appear from LSU Press in 2018.

Mark Irwin's eighth collection of poetry, *American Urn: New & Selected Poems (1987–2014)* was published in 2015. *A Passion According to Green* will appear from New Issues in spring of 2017. He has also translated two volumes of poetry. Recognition for his work includes *The Nation* / Discovery Award, two Colorado Book Awards, four Pushcart Prizes, the James Wright Poetry Award, and fellowships from the Fulbright, Lilly, NEA, and Wurlitzer Foundations. He is an associate professor in the Ph.D. in Creative Writing & Literature Program at the University of Southern California and lives in Los Angeles and Colorado.

Major Jackson is the author of four collections of poetry: *Roll Deep* (2015, Norton); *Holding Company* (2010, Norton); *Hoops* (2006, Norton); and *Leaving Saturn* (2002, University of Georgia Press). *Holding Company* and *Hoops* were both selected as finalists for an NAACP Image Award in the category of Outstanding Literary Work in Poetry; and *Leaving Saturn*, awarded the Cave Canem Poetry Prize for a first book of poems, was a finalist for the National Book Critics Circle Award in Poetry. He has published poems and essays in *AGNI, American Poetry Review, Callaloo, The New Yorker, Ploughshares, Poetry, Tin House,* and in *Best American Poetry* (2004, 2011). He is a recipient of a Pushcart Prize, a Whiting Writers' Award, and has been honored by the Pew Fellowship in the Arts and the Witter Bynner Foundation in conjunction with the Library of Congress.

Mark Jarman is the author of ten books of poetry, the most recent of which is *Bone Fires: New and Selected Poems* (Sarabande Books, 2011). He has also published two collections of his prose, *The Secret of Poetry* (Story Line Press, 2000) and *Body and Soul: Essays on Poetry* (University of Michigan Press, 2001). He is Centennial Professor of English at Vanderbilt University.

Krzysztof Jaworski was born in Kielce, Poland, in 1966, and has written over a dozen books, including *Irksome Pleasures: Collected Poems 1988–2008* and *To the Marrow*, an avant-garde novel about his experience with cancer. He has also published three monographs on the writing, Soviet imprisonment, and execution of the Futurist poet Bruno Jasienski. In the 1990s Jaworski played a central role in *bruLion*, the magazine that launched the careers of several of Poland's most important post-Communist writers. He has also written avant-garde works for stage and screen. He remains one of the most provocative poets in Poland today.

Amanda Johnston earned a Master of Fine Arts in Creative Writing from Stonecoast at the University of Southern Maine. Her poetry and interviews have appeared in numerous online and print publications, among them, *Kinfolks Quarterly, Muzzle, Pluck!* and the anthologies, *Small Batch, di-ver-city* and *The Ringing Ear: Black Poets Lean South.* The recipient of multiple Artist Enrichment grants from the Kentucky Foundation for Women and the Christina Sergeyevna Award from the Austin International Poetry Festival, she is a member of the Affrilachian Poets and a Cave Canem graduate fellow. She has served on the board of directors for the National Women's Alliance, the Kentucky Women Writers Conference, is a co-founder of Black Poets Speak Out, and founding executive director of Torch Literary Arts.

Poet, translator, essayist & anthologist **Pierre Joris** has published some fifty books, most recently *An American Suite* (Inpatient Press), *Barzakh: Poems 2000–2012* (Black Widow Press); *Breathturn into Timestead: The Collected Later Poetry of Paul Celan* (FSG; ALTA National Translation Award 2015); *A Voice full of Cities: The Collected Essays of Robert Kelly* (Contra Mundum Press 2014); and *The University of California Book of North African Literature. Pierre Joris: Cartographies of the In-between*, essays on Joris' work edited by Peter Cockelbergh, came out in 2012. With Jerome Rothenberg he edited *Poems for the Millennium: The University of California Book of Modern & Postmodern Poetry* vols. 1 & 2. When not on the road, he lives & works in Bay Ridge, Brooklyn, with his wife, performance artist Nicole Peyrafitte. They are currently at work on *Talvera: A Millennium of Occitan Poetry* (Poems for the Millennium, vol. 6).

Marilyn Kallet has published seventeen books, including *The Love That Moves Me*, poetry from Black Widow Press. She has translated Eluard's *Last Love Poems*, Péret's *The Big Game*, and has recently co-edited and co-translated Chantal Bizzini's *Disenchanted City* (with J. Bradford Anderson and Darren Jackson.) Dr. Kallet is Nancy Moore Goslee Professor at the University of Tennessee–Knoxville; and she also teaches poetry workshops for VCCA–France in Auvillar. She has performed her poems on campuses and in theaters across the United States as well as in France and Poland, as a guest of the U.S. Embassy. Marilyn Kallet was inducted into the East Tennessee Literary Hall of Fame in 2005.

Dore Kiesselbach's first collection, *Salt Pier* (2012), received the Agnes Lynch Starrett Prize and includes work selected for Britain's Bridport Prize and the Poetry Society of America's Robert H. Winner Memorial Award. His writing has appeared in *AGNI, FIELD, Poetry, Poetry Review, Stand*, and other magazines. He writes copy and performs freelance editing in Minneapolis.

John Kinsella's new collection of poetry is *Firebreaks* (W. W. Norton, 2016). He is a Fellow of Churchill College, Cambridge University, and Professor of Literature and Sustainability at Curtin University.

David Kirby's collection *The House on Boulevard St.: New and Selected Poems* was a finalist for the National Book Award in 2007. Kirby is the author of *Little Richard: The Birth of Rock 'n' Roll*, which the *Times Literary Supplement of London* called "a hymn of praise to the emancipatory power of nonsense." His forthcoming poetry collection from LSU Press is *Get Up, Please*. davidkirby.com.

Karl Kirchwey is the author of six books of poems, most recently *Mount Lebanon* (Marian Wood/Putnam, 2011), as well as a translation of Paul Verlaine's first book titled *Poems Under Saturn* (Princeton

University Press, 2011). His new manuscript is *Stumbling Blocks: Roman Poems*, and he is working on translations of contemporary Italian poet Giovanni Giudici. A Professor of English at Boston University, he also served as Director of Creative Writing at BU, and in 2010–13 was Andrew Heiskell Arts Director at the American Academy in Rome. He was recently awarded the 2015 Classics Conclave Cato Prize for Poetry from the Institute for Digital Archeology.

Lance Larsen's fourth collection of poems, *Genius Loci*, was recently published by University of Tampa Press. His earlier collections include *Backyard Alchemy* (2009), *In All Their Animal Brilliance* (2005), and *Erasable Walls* (1998). He holds a Ph.D. from the University of Houston. His work appears widely, in such venues as *Georgia Review, Southern Review, Ploughshares, Poetry, River Styx, Orion, The Pushcart Prize Anthology, Best American Poetry 2009, Poetry Daily*, and elsewhere. Four of his essays have been listed as Notable in *Best American Essays*.

Sydney Lea was Poet Laureate of Vermont 2011–2015. His twelfth collection of poems, *No Doubt the Nameless*, is now available from Four Way Books, and his fourth collection of lyrical essays, *What's the Story? Short Takes on a Life Grown Long*, has recently been published by Vermont's Green Writers Press.

Phillis Levin's fifth collection, *Mr. Memory & Other Poems*, was published by Penguin in March 2016. She is the author of four other collections, *Temples and Fields* (University of Georgia Press, 1988), *The Afterimage* (Copper Beech Press, 1995), *Mercury* (Penguin, 2001), and *May Day* (Penguin, 2008), and is editor of *The Penguin Book of the Sonnet* (2001). Her honors include the Poetry Society of America's Norma Farber First Book Award, a Fulbright Scholar Award to Slovenia, the Amy Lowell Poetry Travelling Scholarship, and fellowships from the Guggenheim Foundation, the Bogliasco Foundation, and the National Endowment for the Arts. Her work has appeared in *Poetry, The New Yorker, Paris Review, AGNI, The Atlantic, Southwest Review, Yale Review, The New Republic, Literary Imagination, Kenyon Review,* and *The Best American Poetry* (1989, 1998, and 2009 editions). She teaches at Hofstra University and lives in New York City.

Timothy Liu's most recent book of poems is *Don't Go Back To Sleep*. For his upcoming sabbatical, he will be retracing the Mormon trail. timothyliu.net

Luljeta Lleshanaku is internationally known as the most important and inventive Albanian poet of her generation. A winner of the International Kristal Vilenica Prize in 2009, she is the author of seven books of poetry in Albanian and six poetry collections in other languages. *Negative Space* won the 2013 Author of the Year Award from the Publishers Association at the Tirana Book Fair, Albania. Her American collection *Child of Nature* (New Directions, 2010) was a 2011 Best Translated Book Award poetry finalist, and her British collection *Haywire: New & Selected Poems* was nominated for the 2013 Popescu Prize by the Poetry Society, UK.

William Logan's most recent book of poetry is *Strange Flesh* (Penguin, 2008). A volume of new poems, *Madame X*, is out this fall. He has published eight books of poetry and five of essays and reviews. *The Undiscovered Country* won the National Book Critics Circle Award in Criticism. He teaches at the University of Florida and lives in Gainesville, Florida, and Cambridge, England.

James Longenbach is the author of five books of poems, including *Earthling*, which will be published by W. W. Norton in 2017. His poems and reviews appear regularly in *The Nation*, the *New Yorker*, and the *New York Times Book Review*, and his most recent books of criticism are *The Art of the Poetic Line* and *The Virtues of Poetry*, both published by Graywolf Press. He is the Joseph Henry Gilmore Professor of English at the University of Rochester.

Thomas Lux was born in Massachusetts in December 1946 and graduated from Emerson College. He has been awarded grants and fellowships from the Guggenheim Foundation and the Mellon Foundation. He is a three-time recipient of NEA grants. In 1994, he was awarded the Kinglsey Tufts Prize for his book *Split Horizon*. The most recent of his twelve full-length poetry collections is *Child Made of Sand* (Houghton Mifflin Harcourt, 2012). He also recently published *From the Southland* (Marick Press, 2012, nonfiction). BloodAxe Books will bring out *Selected Poems* in the UK in 2014. A book of poems, *Zehntausend Herrliche Jahre*, in German, trs. Klaus Martens, was published in early 2011. Currently, he is Bourne Professor of Poetry and Director of the McEver Visiting Writers program at the Georgia Institute of Technology, as well as Director of Poetry @ Tech.

Maurice Manning's sixth book of poems, *One Man's Dark*, will be published by Copper Canyon in the fall of 2016. Manning's first book, Lawrence Booth's *Book of Visions* was selected by W. S. Merwin for the Yale Series of Younger Poets. His fourth book, *The Common Man*, was a finalist for the Pulitzer Prize. Manning teaches at Transylvania University and in the MFA Program for Writers at Warren Wilson College. He and his family live on a small farm in Kentucky.

Gail Mazur is author of seven books of poems, including *They Can't Take That Away from Me*, finalist for the 2001 National Book Award; *Zeppo's First Wife: New and Selected Poems*, winner of the 2006 Massachusetts Book Award and finalist for the LA Times Book Prize; and *Figures in a Landscape* (2011). *Forbidden City* will appear in 2016 from University of Chicago Press. She is the founding director of the Blacksmith House Poetry Series in Cambridge, a center for the poetry community since 1973 and Distinguished Writer in Residence in the Emerson College Graduate Writing Program and co-founder, with her late husband, Michael Mazur, of Artists Against Racism and War. On the Writing Committee of the Fine Arts Work Center in Provincetown, she has been a Fellow in Poetry at the Bunting Institute and at Radcliffe Institute.

Shane McCrae's most recent book is *The Animal Too Big to Kill* (forthcoming from Persea Books). He teaches at Oberlin College and

Spalding University, and has received a Whiting Writer's Award and a fellowship from the NEA. He lives in Oberlin, Ohio.

Campbell McGrath is the author of many books of poetry, most recently the chapbook *Picasso/Mao* (Upper Rubber Boot, 2014) and *XX: Poem for the 20th Century* (Ecco Press, 2016). He lives in Miami Beach and teaches in the MFA program at Florida International University.

Nancy Mitchell, a 2012 Pushcart Prize recipient, is the author of two volumes of poetry: *The Near Surround* and *Grief Hut*. Her poems have appeared in *Agni, Poetry Daily, Salt Hill Journal*, and *Green Mountains Review*.

Emmanuel Moses was born in Casablanca in 1959. He spent his early childhood in France, lived in Israel for fifteen years, and then returned to Paris, where he still lives. He is the author of twelve collections of poems, most recently *Sombre comme le temps* (Gallimard, 2014) and *Ce qu'il y a à vivre* (La Feugraie, 2012), and of nine novels and prose texts. He is a past recipient of the Prix Mallarmé and a Prix de poésie de l'Académie Française. He is also a translator of contemporary Hebrew fiction and poetry, notably of Yehuda Amichai. Two collections of Moses' poems in Marilyn Hacker's translation were published in the Oberlin College Press *FIELD* Translation Series: *He and I* in 2009 and *Preludes and Fugues* in 2016.

Carol Muske-Dukes is the author of 8 books of poems, four novels, two essay collections & has co-edited anthologies. Her books have been *NY Times* Most Notable Books & she has been a National Book Award finalist, *LA Times* Book Prize finalist, Castagnola Award, Dylan Thomas prize, six Pushcarts, Guggenheim, Barnes & Noble Writer for Writers award. She was California Poet Laureate 2008–2011, poetry columnist for the *LA Times*—also writes for the *NY Times* and *The New Yorker*. She is professor of English/Creative Writing at the University of Southern California, where she founded the Ph.D. Program in Creative Writing/

Literature. She is currently making a film, with others, based on the ancient Greek poet Sappho as a time traveler. carolmuskedukes.com

Duane Niatum has been writing poems, stories and essays for over 50 years. He has been widely published in the US and abroad. He published eight books of poems; most recently, *The Pull of the Green Kite* was published by Serif and Pixel Press in 2011. Duane's writing is deeply connected with the Northwest coast landscape, its mountains, forests, water and creatures. The legends and traditions of his ancestors, who have long called this place home, help shape and animate his poetry. He has published hundreds of poems and dozens of stories in magazines and anthologies in the USA and Europe. He was four times nominated for a Pushcart Prize and has finished a manuscript of his collected poems. He is sending around to the publishers two collections of short stories. Several of his essays on American Indian literature and art have been published in the U.S. and Europe. His poems, stories, and essays were translated into fourteen languages. He has a Ph.D. in American Studies from the University of Michigan/ Ann Arbor. Duane is an enrolled member of the Jamestown S'Klallam tribe. He was invited to read at the Library of Congress and the International Poetry Festival in Rotterdam, the Netherlands. Duane has made a life-long study of art and artists, including American Indian art, literature and culture. He brings unique insight to his writings and publications.

D. Nurkse is the author of ten poetry collections, most recently *A Night in Brooklyn*, which Knopf will reissue in paperback in 2016. He's the recipient of a Literature Award from the American Academy of Arts and Letters.

William Olsen most recent collection of poetry is *Sand Theory*. He teaches in the MFA and Ph.D. programs at Western Michigan University. He edits *New Issues Poetry and Prose*. He lives in Kalamazoo.

Dzvinia Orlowsky is a poet and translator. She is the author of five collections of poetry published by Carnegie Mellon University Press including *A Handful of Bees*, reprinted in 2009 as a Carnegie Mellon Classic Contemporary; *Convertible Night, Flurry of Stones*, recipient of a 2010 Sheila Motton Book Award; and her most recent, *Silvertone*, for which she was named Ohio Poetry Day Association's 2014 Co-Poet of the Year. Her translation from Ukrainian of Alexander Dovzhenko's novella, *The Enchanted Desna*, was published by House Between Water in 2006; and Jeff Friedman's and her translation of *Memorials* by Polish poet Mieczyslaw Jastrun was published by Dialogos in 2014. She is a Founding Editor of Four Way Books, a recipient of a Pushcart Prize, a Massachusetts Cultural Council poetry grant, and recipient with Jeff Friedman of a 2016 National Endowment for the Arts Translation Grant. She teaches at the Solstice Low-Residency MFA for Creative Writing Program of Pine Manor College; as Special Lecturer in Creative Writing at Providence College; and serves as Editor for Poetry in Translation for *Solstice Literary Magazine*.

Alicia Ostriker is a poet and critic. Her thirteenth poetry collection, *The Book of Seventy*, received the 2009 National Jewish Book Award for Poetry; *The Book of Life: Selected Jewish Poems 1979–2011* received a Paterson Lifetime Achievement Award in 2013. She has also received awards from the Poetry Society of America, the San Francisco Poetry Center, the Guggenheim foundation and the Rockefeller Foundation among others, and has twice been a National Book Award finalist. Her most recent book of poems is *The Old Woman, the Tulip, and the Dog*. As a critic, Ostriker is the author of *Stealing the Language: the Emergence of Women's Poetry in America*, and has published several other books on poetry and on the Bible. She is Professor Emerita of Rutgers University, lives in Princeton, NJ, and NYC, and teaches in the Low-Residency MFA Program of Drew University.

Ruth Padel's latest collection *Learning to Make an Oud in Nazareth* addresses creativity, conflict and the Middle East "Wonderful, audacious, minutely crafted: The magnificent central section in the crucifixion is a great imaginative feat" (*Observer*). "An exquisite image-maker who can work wonders with the great tradition of line and stanza" (Colm

Toibin). Ruth is a Fellow of the Royal Society of Literature and teaches Creative Writing at King's College London. ruthpadel.com

Benjamin Paloff is the author of two collections of poems, *And His Orchestra* (2015) and *The Politics* (2011), and his poems have appeared in *A Public Space, The Paris Review, The New Republic*, and elsewhere. A former poetry editor at *Boston Review* and a regular contributor to *The Nation*, he has translated several books from Polish and Czech, including, most recently, Richard Weiner's *The Game for Real* (2015). He has twice received grants from the National Endowment for the Arts—in poetry as well as translation—and has been a fellow of the US Fulbright Programs and the Stanford Humanities Center, among others. He teaches at the University of Michigan.

Linda Pastan's fourteenth book, *Insomnia*, has recently been published by W. W. Norton. She is a former Poet Laureate of Maryland, and in 2003 she won the Ruth Lily Prize for lifetime achievement.

Molly Peacock is the author of seven volumes of poetry, including *The Analyst* (forthcoming) as well as *The Second Blush* and *Cornucopia* (all from W. W. Norton). Her poetry is widely anthologized, appearing in *The Oxford Book of American Poetry* as well as in leading literary journals such as *Poetry* and *The TLS*. She is the co-editor of *Poetry in Motion: 100 Poems from the Subways and Buses* and the Series Editor for *The Best Canadian Poetry in English*. She is also the author of the best-selling *The Paper Garden: Mrs. Delany Begins Her Life's Work at 72*, a biography and meditation on late-life creativity. Recently she has worked with illustrator Kara Kosaka on *Alphabetique: 26 Characteristic Fictions*.

Carl Phillips is the author of thirteen books of poems, most recently *Reconnaissance* (FSG, 2015) and *Silverchest* (FSG, 2013). Phillips has also published two books of prose, *The Art of Daring: Risk, Restlessness, Imagination* and *Coin of the Realm: Essays on the Life and Art of Poetry*, and he is a translator of Sophocles's *Philoctetes*. His awards include the

Los Angeles Times Book Prize for Poetry, the Kingsley Tufts Award, the Theodore Roethke Memorial Foundation Award, the Lambda Literary Award for Gay Poetry, the Thom Gunn Award for Gay Male Poetry, as well as fellowships from the Guggenheim Foundation, the Library of Congress, and the Academy of American Poets. A member of the American Academy of Arts and Sciences, as well as the judge for the Yale Younger Poets Series, Phillips is Professor of English at Washington University in St. Louis.

Gabriel and Marcel Piqueray were identical twins, born in Brussels in 1920. Lovers of jazz and surrealism, they associated with key figures of the movement including André Breton and René Magritte (with whom they held regular "surrealist working meetings" for many years), as well as with the musician Chet Baker and the composer Francis Poulenc. In 1957 they became joint editors of the influential avant-garde journal *Phantomas*, whose contributors included Samuel Beckett, Roland Barthes, René Magritte, Kurt Schwitters, and Jorge Luis Borges, among many others. They published a dozen books (listing "Gabriel and Marcel Piqueray" as authors—the Piqueray brothers did not believe in individual authorship), as well as numerous works in journals, and several works co-authored with Paul Colinet. Gabriel Piqueray died in 1992, Marcel in 1997. *Au-delà des gestes et autres textes*, a selection of their work, was issued by Editions Labor in 1993, and sound recordings of their work were released on the Sub Rosa label in the collection *Le groupe surréaliste révolutionnaire* (Vol 3).

Kevin Prufer's sixth book is *Churches* (Four Way Books, 2014). His seventh, *How He Loved Them*, is forthcoming, also from Four Way Books. Other poems from that collection can be found in *The Paris Review, Poetry, A Public Space, The Southern Review, The Literary Review, FIELD*, and the 2016 *Pushcart Prize Anthology*. With Martha Collins and Martin Rock, he recently edited *Catherine Breese Davis: on the Life & Work of an American Master* for the Unsung Masters Series, which he co-curates.

Lawrence Raab's collection of poems, *What We Don't Know About Each Other*, won the National Poetry Series and was a Finalist for the 1993 National Book Award. Recent books include *The Probable World, Visible Signs: New & Selected Poems*, and *The History of Forgetting*. His newest collection is *Mistaking Each Other for Ghosts* (Tupelo, 2015), which was nominated for the National Book Award, and named one of the ten best poetry books of 2015 by the *New York Times*.

Martha Rhodes is the author of four collections of poetry: *At the Gate* (1995), *Perfect Disappearance* (2000, Green Rose Prize), *Mother Quiet* (2004) and *The Beds* (2012). Her poems have been published widely in such journals as *AGNI, Columbia, Fence, New England Review, Pleiades, Ploughshares, Prairie Schooner, TriQuarterly*, and the *Virginia Quarterly Review*. She has also been anthologized widely, her work appearing in *AGNI 30 Years, Appetite: Food as Metaphor, Extraordinary Tide: New Poetry by American Women, The New American Poets: A Bread Loaf Anthology, Last Call: Poems on Alcoholism, Addiction, and Deliverance*, and *The KGB Bar Book of Poetry*, among others.

Rhodes has taught at Emerson College, New School University, and University of California at Irvine. She currently teaches at Sarah Lawrence College and the MFA Program for Writers at Warren Wilson College. She has been a visiting or guest poet at many colleges and universities around the country and has taught at conferences such as the Fine Arts Work Center in Provincetown, The Frost Place, Indiana University, Sarah Lawrence Summer Conference, and Third Coast. She serves on many publishing panels throughout each year at colleges, conferences and arts organizations, and is a regular guest editor at the Bread Loaf Writers Conference and the Colrain Manuscript Conference. She also teaches private weekly workshops. In 2010, she took over the directorship of the Frost Place Conference on Poetry in Franconia, NH. Rhodes is the director of Four Way Books, publishers of poetry and short fiction, located in New York City.

Susan Rich is the author of four poetry collections including *Cloud Pharmacy, The Alchemist's Kitchen, Cures Include Travel*, and *The*

Cartographer's Tongue: Poems of the World (White Pine). Along with Brian Turner she is a co-editor of *The Strangest of Theatres: Poets Crossing Borders*, and she has received awards from *The Times Literary Supplement*, Peace Corps Writers, PEN USA, Fulbright Foundation and Washington State Book Awards. Rich's poems have appeared in the *Harvard Review, New England Review*, and elsewhere. Her work has been translated into Slovenian and Swedish.

David Rivard's new collection of poems, *Standoff*, will be published by Graywolf in early 2016. His other books include *Otherwise Elsewhere, Sugartown*, and *Wise Poison*, winner of the James Laughlin Prize from the Academy of American Poets and a finalist for the *Los Angeles Times* Book Award. He teaches in the MFA in Writing program at the University of New Hampshire.

Hoyt Rogers divides his time between the Dominican Republic and Italy. His poems, stories, and essays, as well as his translations from the French, German, and Spanish, have appeared in a wide variety of periodicals. He has published over a dozen books, which include his own poetry and criticism as well as editions and translations. His most recent translation from the French, *Second Simplicity*—a collection of verse and prose by Yves Bonnefoy—was published by the Yale University Press in January 2012. With Paul Auster, he published *Openwork*, an André du Bouchet reader, at Yale in 2014. He is currently translating two new works by Bonnefoy for Seagull Books; "The Walk in the Forest" is from one of them, *Together Still*.

Carnegie Mellon just re-published **Ira Sadoff**'s *Palm Reading in Winter* as part of their Contemporary Classics series. Since *True Faith* he has had work in *APR* and *The Kenyon Review* and several anthologies. He lives in a converted barn in upstate NY.

Mary Jo Salter is the author of seven books of poems published by Knopf, including *A Phone Call to the Future: New and Selected Poems* (2008) and *Nothing by Design* (2013). An additional collection, *It's*

Hard to Say: Selected Poems, appeared in the UK from Waywiser Press in 2015. She is a co-editor of *The Norton Anthology of Poetry* and is co-chair of The Writing Seminars at Johns Hopkins University. She lives in Baltimore.

Grace Schulman is the recipient of the Frost Medal for Distinguished Lifetime Achievement in American Poetry, awarded by the Poetry Society of America, 2016. Her seventh book is *Without a Claim* (Houghton Mifflin Harcourt, 2013). Her earlier books include *Paintings of Our Lives, For That Day Only, Hemispheres,* and *Burn Down the Icons.* Her poems have appeared in *The Best American Poetry* and *The Best of the Best American Poetry* and in *Pushcart Prize Anthologies* 21 and 23. She is author of *Marianne Moore: The Poetry of Engagement;* editor of Ezra Pound; translator from the Hebrew of T. Carmi's *At the Stone of Losses;* and co-translator from the Spanish of Pablo Antonio Cuadra's *Songs of Cifar.* Her work has appeared in *The New Yorker, The New Republic, Paris Review, Antaeus, Grand Street, Yale Review, Hudson Review, Kenyon Review,* and elsewhere. She is the former Poetry Editor of *The Nation,* and former Director of the Poetry Center, 92nd Street Y.

Maureen Seaton has authored seventeen poetry collections, both solo and collaborative—most recently, *Fibonacci Batman: New & Selected Poems* (Carnegie Mellon University Press). Her honors include the Iowa Poetry Prize, the Lambda Literary Award, the Publishing Triangle's Audre Lorde Award, the Society of Midland Authors Award, and an NEA Fellowship. Her work has been included in both the *Pushcart Prize Anthology* and *Best American Poetry.* She teaches poetry at the University of Miami.

Martha Serpas has published three collections of poetry, *Côte Blanche, The Dirty Side of the Storm,* and *The Diener.* A native of south Louisiana, she co-produced *Veins in the Gulf,* a documentary about coastal erosion. She teaches at the University of Houston and serves as a hospital trauma chaplain.

Alan Shapiro is the author of twelve books of poetry (including *Night of the Republic*, a finalist for both the National Book Award and The Griffin Prize), two memoirs (*The Last Happy Occasion*, which was a finalist for the National Book Circle Critics Award in autobiography, and *Vigil*), a novel (*Broadway Baby*), a book of critical essays (*In Praise of the Impure: Poetry and the Ethical Imagination*) and two translations (*The Oresteia* by Aeschylus and *The Trojan Women* by Euripides, both published by Oxford University Press). Shapiro has won numerous awards, including The Kingsley Tufts Award, *LA Times* Book Prize, The O.B. Hardison Award from the Folger Shakespeare Library, and The William Carlos Williams Award from the Poetry Society of America. His new book of poems, *Reel to Reel*, was published in April 2014 by University of Chicago Press.

Jeffrey Skinner's most recent collection of poems is *Glaciology*. He is a 2014–2015 Guggenheim Fellow in Poetry, and in 2015 was given a literature award from the American Academy of Arts & Letters. Other recent poems have appeared in *Poetry*, *The Kenyon Review*, and *Forklift*. He trudges the road to happy destiny in Louisville, KY.

Tara Skurtu is a Boston-based poet, teacher, and translator currently living in Romania, where she is a Fulbright lecturer in creative writing. She is the recipient of two Academy of American Poets prizes and a Robert Pinsky Global Fellowship, and her recent poems appear or are forthcoming in *The Kenyon Review*, *Poetry Review*, *Poetry Wales*, *Memorious*, *The Common*, and *Tahoma Literary Review*. She has recently completed her first poetry manuscript, *The Amoeba Game*.

Ron Slate has published two books of poetry, *The Incentive of the Maggot* and *The Great Wave*, both via Houghton Mifflin Harcourt. He reviews poetry and literature at the website On the Seawall and is a board member of Mass Humanities (NEH). He lives in Milton and Aquinnah, MA.

Tom Sleigh's many books include *Army Cats*, winner of the John Updike Award from the American Academy of Arts and Letters, and *Space Walk*, which won the $100,000 Kingsley Tufts Award. In addition, *Far Side of the Earth* won an Academy Award from the American Academy of Arts and Letters, *The Dreamhouse* was a finalist for the Los Angeles Times Book Award, and *The Chain* was a finalist for the Lenore Marshall Prize. His new book, *Station Zed*, was published by Graywolf in 2015. He has also published a book of essays, *Interview With a Ghost*, and a translation of Euripides' *Herakles*. His poems and prose appear in *The New Yorker, Virginia Quarterly Review, Poetry, American Poetry Review, Yale Review, Threepenny Review* and *The Village Voice*, as well as *The Best of the Best American Poetry, The Best American Poetry, Best American Travel Writing*, and the *Pushcart Anthology*. He has received the Shelley Prize from the Poetry Society of America, fellowships from the American Academy in Berlin and the Civitella Ranieri Foundation, and grants from the Lila Wallace Fund, the Guggenheim Foundation and the NEA, among others. He is a Distinguished Professor in the MFA Program at Hunter College and lives in Brooklyn. He also works as a journalist in Syria, Lebanon, Somalia, Kenya, Iraq, and Libya.

Patricia Smith is the author of seven books of poetry, including *Shoulda Been Jimi Savannah*, winner of the 2014 Rebekah Bobbitt Prize from the Library of Congress, the 2013 Lenore Marshall Poetry Prize from the Academy of American Poets and the Phillis Wheatley Award; *Savannah* was a finalist for both the William Carlos Williams Award from the Poetry Society of America and the Balcones Prize. Patricia also authored *Blood Dazzler*, a finalist for the National Book Award, and *Teahouse of the Almighty*, a National Poetry Series selection.

Her most recent book is *Gotta Go Gotta Flow*, a collaboration with the late Chicago photographer Michael Abramson. Her work has appeared in *Poetry, Paris Review, The New York Times, TriQuarterly, Tin House*, the *Washington Post*, and in both *Best American Poetry* and *Best American Essays*. Her contribution to the crime fiction anthology *Staten Island Noir*, which she edited, won the Robert L. Fish Award from the Mystery Writers of America for the best debut story of the year and was chosen for *Best American Mystery Stories*. She is a 2014 Guggenheim fellow, a 2012 fellow at both MacDowell and Yaddo, a two-time Pushcart Prize winner, recipient of a Lannan fellowship and a four-time individual champion of the National Poetry Slam, the most successful poet in the competition's history. Her next poetry collection, tentatively titled *Incendiary Art*, will be released in February 2017; she is also working on a volume combining poetic monologues with 19th-century photos of African Americans, and a collaborative novel with her husband Bruce DeSilva, the Edgar-Award winning author of the Liam Mulligan crime novels. Patricia is a professor at the City University of New York/College of Staten Island and an instructor in the MFA program at Sierra Nevada College.

Ron Smith is the Poet Laureate of Virginia. His book of poems *The Humility of the Brutes* is forthcoming from Louisiana State University Press. His *Its Ghostly Workshop* appeared from LSU in 2013; his *Moon Road: Poems* 1986–2005 appeared from LSU in 2007. His first book, *Running Again in Hollywood Cemetery* (1988), was runner-up for the National Poetry Series Open Competition and the Samuel French Morse Poetry Prize and was subsequently published by University Presses of Florida. Smith is the winner of the Carole Weinstein Poetry Prize, the Guy Owen Award from *Southern Poetry Review*, and the Theodore Roethke Prize from *Poetry Northwest* and has published poems in many magazines and anthologies, including *The Nation, The Georgia Review, The Southern Review, Virginia Quarterly Review, Shenandoah*, and *New England Review*. Smith's critical prose and poetry columns can be found in *The Georgia Review, Blackbird, The Richmond Times-Dispatch, The Kenyon Review, Shenandoah*, and elsewhere.

Lisa Russ Spaar's 's most recent book of poems is *Vanitas, Rough*, and her fifth collection of poems, *Orexia*, is due out from Persea Books in early 2017. Among her edited volumes is the just-released *Monticello in Mind: 50 Contemporary Poems on Jefferson*. Her awards include a Guggenheim Fellowship and a Rona Jaffe Award for Emerging Women Writers. She is professor of English and Creative Writing at the University of Virginia and writes a regular column on second books of poetry for the *Los Angeles Review of Books*.

Maura Stanton was selected by Stanley Kunitz for the Yale Series of Younger Poets Competition for *Snow on Snow* and has published five other books of poetry, most recently *Immortal Sofa* (University of Illinois Press, 2008). She has poems in recent or forthcoming issues of *Ecotone*, *The Southwest Review*, *The Yale Review*, *The Hudson Review*, and *Southern Poetry Review*. Her short story "Oh Shenandoah" appears in *The O'Henry Prize Stories 2014*.

Page Hill Starzinger lives in New York City. Her first full-length poetry book, *Vestigial*, selected by Lynn Emanuel to win the Barrow Street Book Prize, was published in fall 2013. Her chapbook *Unshelter*, selected by Mary Jo Bang as winner of the Noemi contest, was published in 2009. Her poems have appeared in *Colorado Review*, *Fence*, *Kenyon Review*, *Pleiades*, *Volt* and many others.

Terese Svoboda's *When The Next Big War Blows Down The Valley: Selected and New Poems* (Anhinga Press) was published in 2015, *Anything that Burns You: A Portrait of Lola Ridge, Radical Poet* (Schaffner Press) in February 2016, and *Professor Harriman's Steam Air-Ship* (Eyewear) will appear in October. *Live Sacrifice*, her book of short stories, will be published in 2017.

Brian Swann's most recent publications are *Dogs on the Roof* (MadHat Press, 2016), prose; *St. Francis and the Flies* (Autumn House Press, 2016), poetry; *Sky Loom: Native American Myth, Story, and Song* (University of Nebraska Press, 2014); and *In Late Light* (Johns Hopkins University Press, 2013), poetry. Sheep Meadow Press will publish *Companions, Analogies* (poetry) this fall.

Cole Swensen is the author of fifteen volumes of poetry, most recently *Landscapes on a Train* (Nightboat Books, 2015) and *Gravesend* (U. of

California Press, 2012), and a volume of essays, *Noise That Stays Noise* (U. of Michigan Press, 2011.

Arthur Sze's books of poetry include *Compass Rose* (Copper Canyon, 2014), *The Ginkgo Light, Quipu,* and *The Redshifting Web.* A professor emeritus at the Institute of American Indian Arts, as well as a chancellor of the Academy of American Poets, he lives in Santa Fe, NM.

Adam Tavel is the author of *Plash & Levitation* (University of Alaska Press, 2015), winner of the Permafrost Book Prize, and *The Fawn Abyss* (Salmon Poetry, 2016). adamtavel.com

Daniel Tobin is the author of seven books of poems, *Where the World Is Made, Double Life, The Narrows, Second Things, Belated Heavens, The Net,* and the book-length poem *From Nothing.* His critical studies include *Passage to the Center: Imagination and the Sacred in the Poetry of Seamus Heaney* and *Awake in America.* He is the editor of *The Book of Irish American Poetry from the Eighteenth Century to the Present, Poet's Work, Poet's Play: Essays on the Practice and the Art* (with Pimone Triplett), and *Light in Hand: The Selected Early Poems of Lola Ridge. The Collected Early Poems of Lola Ridge* will be published in 2016. Among his awards are the Discovery/*The Nation* Award, The Robert Penn Warren Award, the Robert Frost Fellowship, the Katherine Bakeless Nason Prize, the Massachusetts Book Award in Poetry, and creative writing fellowships from the National Endowment for the Arts and the John Simon Guggenheim Foundation.

Marc Vincenz is the author of eight collections of poetry; his latest is *Becoming the Sound of Bees* (2015, Ampersand Books). Vincenz is also the translator of many German-language poets, including Herman Hesse Prize winner, Klaus Merz, but also Werner Lutz, Erica Burkart and Jürg Amman, and has published seven collections of translations—the latest is *A Late Recognition of the Signs* by Erica Burkart. His translation of Klaus Merz's collection, *Unexpected Development,* was a finalist for the 2015 Cliff Becker Book Translation Prize. He has received several grants from the Swiss Arts Council and a fellowship from the Literarisches Colloquium Berlin. His own work has been translated into German, Russian, Romanian, French, Icelandic and Chinese. Recent and forthcoming publications include *The Nation, Ploughshares, Washington Square Review, The Common,* and *World Literature Today.*

Among **Arthur Vogelsang**'s books of poetry are *A Planet* (Holt, 1983), *Cities and Towns* (University of Massachusetts Press, 1996), and the forthcoming *Orbit* (University of Pittsburgh Press, 2016). He has appeared numerous times in *The Best American Poetry, The New Yorker, Poetry, The Pushcart Prize, Volt,* and *Zocalo Public Square.* arthurvogelsang.com

Connie Voisine is the author of three books of poems including *Calle Florista* (University of Chicago Press, 2015). She has poems published in *The New Yorker, The Georgia Review, Ploughshares, Poetry, Black Warrior Review, Threepenny Review*, and elsewhere. Voisine teaches in the creative writing program at New Mexico State University.

G. C. Waldrep's most recent books are a long poem, *Testament* (BOA Editions, 2015), and a chapbook, *Susquehanna* (Omnidawn, 2013). With Joshua Corey he edited *The Arcadia Project: North American Postmodern Pastoral* (Ahsahta, 2012). He lives in Lewisburg, PA, where he teaches at Bucknell University, edits the journal *West Branch*, and serves as Editor-at-Large for *The Kenyon Review.*

Afaa Michael Weaver's recent awards include the 2014 Kingsley Tufts Award, his fourth Pushcart prize in the 40th anniversary *Pushcart Prize Anthology*, inclusion in *The Best American Poetry* 2014, 2015, and the 2015 Phillis Wheatley Book Award in Poetry from the Harlem Book Fair. His latest book is *City of Eternal Spring* (U. of Pitt, 2014). Afaa teaches at Simmons College and in the MFA program at Drew University.

Scott Withiam's first book, *Arson & Prophets*, was published by Ashland Poetry Press. His poems are recently out in *Ascent, Antioch Review, Barrow Street, Beloit Poetry Journal, Chattahoochee Review, Cimarron Review, Diagram, The Literary Review, Plume, Salamander* and *Western Humanities Review*. He works for a non-profit in the Boston area.

Geoffrey Young has lived in Great Barrington, MA, since 1982. He spent student years in Santa Barbara (UCSB), and Albuquerque (UNM), then lived for two years in Paris (a Fulbright year followed by a six-month stint working for La Galerie Sonnabend). His small press, The Figures (1975–2005), published more than 135 books of poetry, art writing, and fiction.

His own recent books include *Sixteen Candles*, with images by Mark Olshansky, 2016; *Propitious*, with images by Lisa Sylvester, 2016; *Sapphire Drive*, 2015; and *The Point Less Taken*, 2013, with images by Lucas Reiner. He has directed the Geoffrey Young Gallery for the last 24 years, as well as written catalog essays for a dozen artists.

Sa'adi Youssef was born near Basra, Iraq, in 1934. He started writing poetry at the age of seventeen and has published thirty-two collections, a volume of short stories, two novels, several essays, and four volumes of his collected works. Twice exiled from Iraq, he lived in many countries before settling in the UK. He has translated major international poets into Arabic, including Walt Whitman, C. P. Cavafy, Yannis Ritsos, Federico Garcia Lorca, Vasco Popa and Ungaretti. His first major English collection *Without an Alphabet, Without a Face*, translated by Khaled Mattawa, was published in 2002 by Graywolf.

hello
hello

muji   muji.com

Mooji

CPSIA information can be obtained
at www.ICGtesting.com
Printed in the USA
FSOW04n1134091116
27101FS